Physical Science

by Deborah Crotts

illustrated by Joe Dolce

cover design by Jeff Van Kanegan

Publisher
Instructional Fair • TS Denison
Grand Rapids, Michigan 49544

About the Author

Deborah Crotts currently teaches fourth grade and is in charge of revising the entire science curriculum for her school. She has enjoyed working with children at different age levels during her many varied teaching assignments. Deborah's published writing includes numerous magazine articles and six teacher resource books for middle school teachers. She and her family currently live in Gibsonville, North Carolina.

Instructional Fair • TS Denison grants the individual purchaser permission to reproduce the student activity materials in this book for noncommercial individual or classroom use only. Reproduction for an entire school or school system is strictly prohibited. No part of this publication may be reproduced for storage in a retrieval system, or transmitted in any form or by any means, electronic, mechanical, recording, or otherwise, without the prior written permission of the publisher. For information regarding permission, write to Instructional Fair • TS Denison, P.O. Box 1650, Grand Rapids, MI 49501.

ISBN: 1-56822-460-5
Physical Science
Copyright © 1997 by Instructional Fair • TS Denison
2400 Turner Avenue NW
Grand Rapids, Michigan 49544

All Rights Reserved • Printed in the USA

Table of Contents

Measuring 1
Measurement Charts 2
Lab Tools 3
Matter 4
Substances 5
Combining Substances 6
Atoms 7
What Do Atoms Look Like? 8
What Do These Letters Mean? 9
The Elements 10
Atomic Numbers 11
The Periodic Table 12
Molecules 14
Ions 15
What Is Special About Ions 16
Organic Compounds 17
Chemical Equations 18
Solutions 19
Electrolytes 20
Concentrations 21
Making Crystals 22
Chemical Reactions 23
Catalysts 24
Qualitative Analysis 25
Acids 26
Bases 27
Precipitates 28
Isotopes 29
Force 30
Magnetism 31
Electromagnets 32
Other Kinds of Force 33
Are Forces Always Balanced? 34
The Laws of Motion 35
Motion 36
The Theory of Relativity 37
Work 38
Simple Machines 39
Using Simple Machines 40
Can a Machine Be More Efficient? . . . 41

Energy 42
Different Forms of Energy 43
Electric Charge 45
Static Electricity 46
Conductors 47
Electric Current 48
Circuits 49
Measuring Electricity 50
Waves 51
Light 53
Lenses 54
Reflections 55
Interference 56
Answer Key 57

About This Book

The activities and experiments in *Physical Science* are safe and fun and are designed to be a review of the basic facts of physical science as well as a challenge to students.

The book is set up as a progression of skills in physical science, starting with the basic skills of measurement and the concepts of matter, atoms, elements, work, machines, and forces. More advanced concepts such as Einstein's theory of relativity are also covered. A student may start at the front of the book and work to the back or use the table of contents to choose special areas of interest.

Each experiment requires easily obtainable and inexpensive materials and is safe to perform with a minimum of adult supervision. Activities and experiments are fully explained with accompanying background information to supplement the topic and aid in understanding. The activities are self-explanatory and may be used independently of one another. They require no previous knowledge of physical science.

Use the information in the book as a launching point for further research and experiments. Science is an active, ongoing process. Students learn to be scientists by asking questions and searching for the answers. Experiments with lenses led Galileo to the telescope. The keys to future space travel, time travel, and a million new inventions lie in the information we now know. An answer key for each activity question is found in the back of the book to help the learner check his or her understanding.

Measuring

In many countries, the metric system is the standard of measurement at work, in the laboratory, and at home. In the United States, we use a system of measurement called the United States Conventional System. Our system is based on the British Imperial System of measurement. The metric system was developed by a group of French scientists appointed to a special French National Assembly during the time of the French Revolution. It is a decimal system which makes it easy to convert one unit to another. Thomas Jefferson tried to convince Congress to adopt the metric system and failed. Several other attempts have been made to get our country to "go metric," but our own system remains firmly in place for everyday measurement.

Compare a yardstick and a meter stick (length), a one-liter bottle and a quart bottle (volume), and an ounce of sugar and a gram of sugar (weight) to see the size differences between the two systems. Which units are bigger in each case?

_____

To see why scientists prefer the metric system, try these problems using the different systems. Use the charts on the facing page to answer each question.

1. Susie has measured her room with a tape measure to find out how much wallpaper border she needs. She needs 624 inches of border paper. Border paper is sold by the foot. How many feet of border paper does she need? _____

2. Harry wanted to practice for a three-kilometer race. He measured his yard and found that the perimeter of his yard was 1,000 meters long. How many times must he run around the perimeter to run three kilometers? _____

3. Judy is making ice cream. She wants to double the recipe, which calls for three quarts of milk. She has only a cup to measure with. How many cups will she need for six quarts of milk? _____

4. Max needs one liter of oil. He has three half-empty containers. Two contain 300 milliliters of oil and one contains 400 milliliters of oil. How many liters of oil is in the half-empty containers? _____

Which problems are easier to solve? Why? _____

_____

Measurement Charts

United States Conventional System

12 inches = 1 foot
3 feet = 1 yard
5,280 feet = 1 mile

2 cups = 1 pint
2 pints = 1 quart
4 quarts = 1 gallon

16 ounces = 1 pound
1 ton = 2,000 pounds

Metric Measurement

Volume
1 liter = 1,000 milliliters
1 liter = 100 centiliters
1 liter = 10 deciliters
10 liters = 1 dekaliter
100 liters = 1 hectoliter
1,000 liters = 1 kiloliter

Weight
1 gram = 1,000 milligrams
1 gram = 100 centigrams
1 gram = 10 decigrams
10 grams = 1 dekagram
100 grams = 1 hectogram
1000 grams = 1 kilogram

Length
1 meter = 1,000 millimeters
1 meter = 100 centimeters
1 meter = 10 decimeters
10 meters = 1 dekameter
100 meters = 1 hectometer
1000 meters = 1 kilometer

In the metric system of measurement, the prefix tells you what part of the unit you have.

The prefix **deci-** means ⅒ of a unit.
1. What does the prefix **centi-** mean? _____ of the unit.
2. What does the prefix **milli-** mean? _____ of the unit.

The prefix **deka-** means ten times the unit.
3. What does the prefix **hecto-** mean? _____ the unit.
4. What does the prefix **kilo-** mean? _____ the unit.

Lab Tools

In the laboratory, you use several tools and instruments that are similar to, but not the same as, items you might have at home. Look at the descriptions on the left and the pictures on the right and match the letters of the items with the correct descriptions.

1. The *balance* is used to weigh something. The item being weighed is placed on the balance pan and the weights are added or removed until the pan balances or is level. _____

2. *Tongs* are used to hold hot or extremely cold items or items that cannot be picked up by hand. _____

3. A *graduated cylinder* is sometimes called a graduate. It is a tall, slender cylinder used to measure the volume of liquids. _____

4. A *ring stand* is a tall metal pole on a stand. It is used to hold something off the ground or table. _____

5. A *test tube* is used for mixing, heating, cooling, and observing chemicals or other items. _____

6. A *test tube clamp* can be attached to a test tube and then clamped to a ring stand to keep a test tube off of the ground or table. _____

7. A *Bunsen burner* is used to heat chemicals. A Bunsen burner should *never* be used without adult supervision. _____

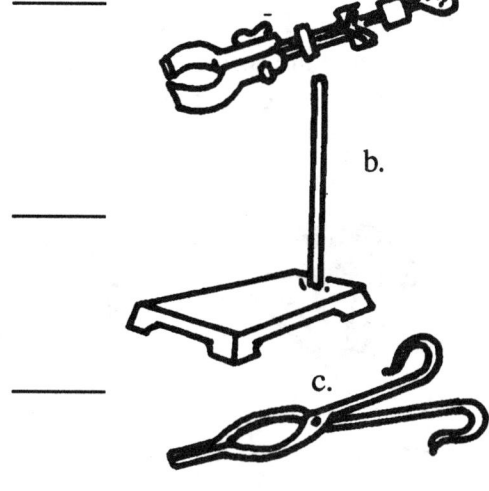

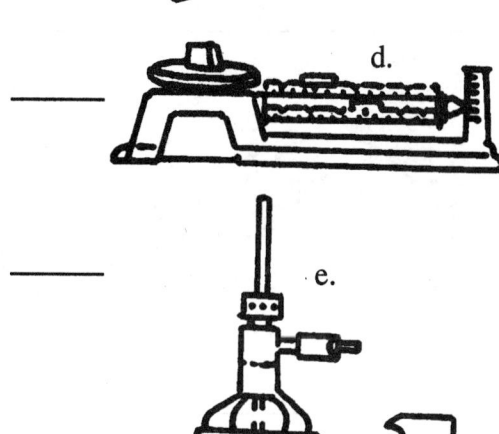

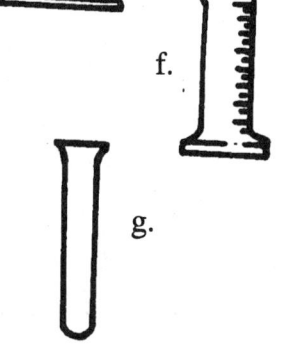

a.

b.

c.

d.

e.

f.

g.

© Instructional Fair • TS Denison   IF2716 Physical Science

Matter

Matter is anything that occupies space and has *mass*. Everything in the universe is made of matter. Matter occurs in one of three states—*solid, liquid,* or *gas.* A *solid* has definite shape and definite *volume.* A *liquid* has a definite volume, but it takes the shape of its container. A *gas* has no definite shape and no definite volume. A gas conforms to the shape and size of its container. It can be compressed to fit a small container and will expand to fill a large container. Look at the pictures below. Some of these things are matter and some are not. Some are solids or liquids or gases. Label each picture **M** for matter or **NT** for not matter. Label each kind of matter with its correct state—*solid, liquid,* or *gas.*

1. _____

2. _____

3. _____

4. _____

5. _____

6. _____

7. _____

8. _____

9. _____

Substances

Most matter is composed of a combination of different *pure substances*. A pure substance is matter that has a fixed composition and distinct properties. For example, water is a substance. It is composed of the *elements* hydrogen and oxygen. Elements are substances that cannot be broken down into any simpler substances by chemical means. Water can contain many other things—salt (as in seawater), dissolved minerals, and other impurities.

Every substance has *physical properties* and *chemical properties*. The physical properties are the color, the odor, the density, the boiling point, the melting point, the hardness or softness, and any other properties that describe the substance. The chemical properties of a substance tell how a substance may change or react with other substances. For example, how will a substance burn? Does the substance rust or oxidize? Will the substance dissolve in water? Study the illustrations below. Tell whether each thing is a substance or an element and what its physical properties are. A chemical property is given for each item.

Salt - sodium chloride.
Chemical property = water soluble

Gold
Chemical property = not water soluble

_____   _____
_____   _____
_____   _____

The changes that substances undergo can be classified as physical or chemical changes. In a physical change, the substance changes its appearance, but can be changed back to its original state. For instance, water can be frozen to ice and melted back to water. This is a physical change. In a chemical change, the composition of the substance has been changed. If you fry an egg, you cannot change it back to the raw egg inside the shell. Label the changes below "C" for chemical change or "P" for physical change.

_____ ice cream melted   _____ log burned

_____ water evaporated   _____ pancake cooked

Combining Substances

If two or more substances are combined and each substance stays the same, the combination is called a mixture. If the mixture has the same composition and appearance throughout, it is called a solution. Salt and pepper stirred together are a mixture. Salt and water stirred together are a solution. In both cases, you can separate the two substances. You can pick the pepper flakes out of the salt, and you can evaporate or boil off the water to leave the salt. An *element* is a substance that cannot be separated into simpler substances by chemical means. A *compound* is a combination of two or more elements which can be separated by chemical means but cannot be separated any other way. An example of a compound is water. Water can be separated into hydrogen and oxygen, which are both elements, but they must be separated by chemical means. You cannot pick the oxygen apart from the hydrogen with tweezers or boil off the hydrogen and leave the oxygen. Read the descriptions below. In the blank beside each substance, mark whether it is a mixture, a solution, an element, or a compound.

Sugar is a combination of carbon, oxygen, and hydrogen.

Mercury is a silver-colored metal. It is a liquid at room temperature and is used in thermometers.

Cinnamon and sugar is a combination of sugar and the spice, cinnamon.

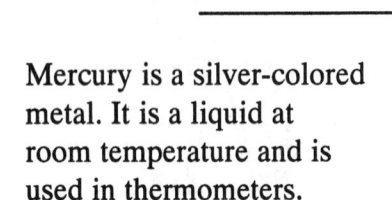

Sugar water is a good food for hummingbirds. Water combined with plain sugar will nourish the birds; red coloring is not necessary.

Atoms

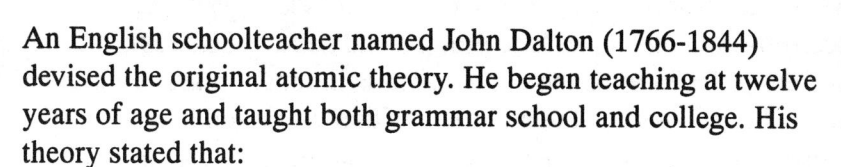

An English schoolteacher named John Dalton (1766-1844) devised the original atomic theory. He began teaching at twelve years of age and taught both grammar school and college. His theory stated that:

1. An element is composed of tiny particles called atoms.

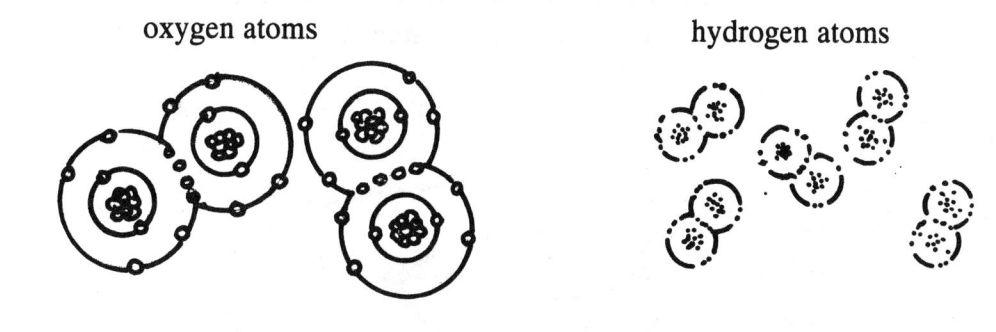

   oxygen atoms   hydrogen atoms

2. The atoms of each kind of element are identical. (The oxygen atoms look like other oxygen atoms, but are different from hydrogen atoms.)

3. Atoms of different elements have different properties.

    a. What does gold look like? _____

    b. What does silver look like? _____

4. Atoms of one element cannot be changed into atoms of another element by chemical reactions, and elements are not created or destroyed by chemical reactions.

5. When the atoms of two or more kinds of elements are combined, a compound is formed.

    a. When you combine oxygen and hydrogen, you get what compound? _____

    b. How is this compound different from both hydrogen and oxygen? _____

What Do Atoms Look Like?

Atoms are composed of three primary particles—*protons, neutrons,* and *electrons*. The protons and neutrons share the nucleus, the center of the atom which is the main mass of the atom. The nucleus of the atom is positively charged because protons are positively charged particles and neutrons have no charge. The protons and neutrons are of about equal size. The electrons give the atom its size, but they are tiny, lightweight particles with a negative charge. They orbit the nucleus of the atom. Atoms actually look more like the blades of a rapidly moving fan; they are a blurry cloud. Label protons, neutrons, and electrons in the Bohr diagram below.

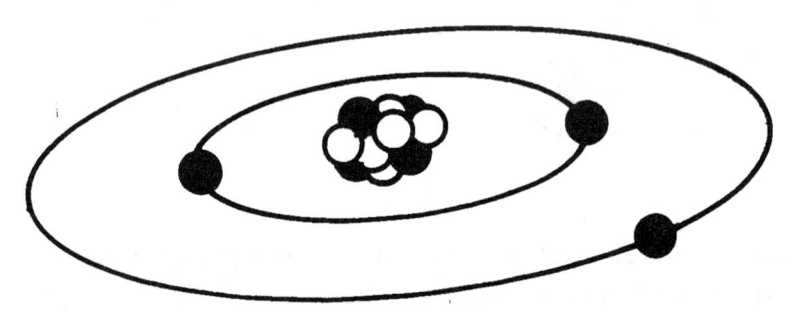

1. Since the number of positively charged protons in an atom is equal to the number of negatively charged electrons, what is the net electric charge of an atom? _____

An atom is incredibly small. The largest atom is 4×10^{-22}g. The actual measurement for the mass of an atom is called the atomic mass unit or amu. One amu is equal to 1.66053×10^{-24}g. In other words, if you put 10,000,000,000,000,000,000,000,000 atoms of this size in a cup, they would weigh 1.66053 grams.

Another unit of measurement for the atom is the *angstrom*.

One angstrom equals 10^{-10}m. In other words, if you laid 100,000,000,000 atoms with this diameter side by side, the total would equal one meter in length.

2. A chlorine atom is 2.0 angstroms in diameter. How many would you need to place edge to edge to equal one meter in length? _____

What Do These Letters Mean?

When scientists write chemical equations or label bottles of chemicals, they do not use the long name for each element. They use an abbreviation of the name called a *chemical symbol* for each element. For example, oxygen is written as O. Sometimes, when two elements unite to form a molecule of a compound, the atoms link up in threes or groups which have more of one element than another. For instance, to form water, two hydrogen atoms link up with one oxygen atom. The *chemical formula* for water is H_2O. Since there are two hydrogen atoms for every oxygen atom, a little number two is written to the right of and slightly below the H which is the chemical symbol for hydrogen. Use the chart on the next page to find the chemical symbols for the following elements.

Silver _____   Carbon _____   Tin _____

Chlorine _____   Boron _____   Arsenic _____

Argon _____   Sulfur _____   Platinum _____

Helium _____   Radon _____   Neon _____

What are the elements in the following compounds? How many atoms of each element are in one molecule of each compound?

Ammonium nitrate: $N H_4 N O_2$ _____

_____

Potassium Chlorate: $K Cl O_3$ _____

_____

Sodium Peroxide: $Na_2 O_2$ _____

_____

Sulfuric Acid: $H S O_4$ _____

_____

Alka-Seltzer: $Na H C O_3$ _____

_____

Tums: $Ca C O_3$ _____

_____

© Instructional Fair • TS Denison   IF2716 Physical Science

The Elements

The known elements are listed below. Beside each name is a single letter or a pair of letters. This is the chemical symbol for the element. Many of the elements have symbols that do not seem to relate to the name of the element. The symbols for these elements often come from Latin names for these elements. For instance, the chemical symbol for gold is **Au**, which stands for *aurium*, the Latin word for gold. The chemical symbol follows the name of each element below. The number immediately to the right of the symbol is the atomic number.

Actinium	Ac	89	Holmium	Ho	67	Rhodium	Rh	45
Aluminum	Al	13	Hydrogen	H	1	Rubidium	Rb	37
Americium	Am	95	Indium	In	49	Ruthenium	Ru	44
Antimony	Sb	51	Iodine	I	53	Rutherfordium	*Rf	104
Argon	Ar	18	Iridium	Ir	77	Samarium	Sm	62
Arsenic	As	33	Iron	Fe	26	Scandium	Sc	21
Astatine	At	85	Krypton	Kr	36	Selenium	Se	34
Barium	Ba	56	Lanthanum	La	57	Silicon	Si	14
Berkelium	Bk	97	Lawrencium	Lr	103	Silver	Ag	47
Beryllium	Be	4	Lead	Pb	82	Sodium	Na	11
Bismuth	Bi	83	Lithium	Li	3	Strontium	Sr	38
Boron	B	5	Lutetium	Lu	71	Sulfur	S	16
Bromine	Br	35	Magnesium	Mg	12	Tantalum	Ta	73
Cadmium	Cd	48	Manganese	Mn	25	Technetium	Tc	43
Calcium	Ca	20	Mendelevium	Md	101	Tellurium	Te	52
Californium	Cf	98	Mercury	Hg	80	Terbium	Tb	65
Carbon	C	6	Molybdenum	Mo	42	Thallium	Tl	81
Cerium	Ce	58	Neodymium	Nd	60	Thorium	Th	90
Cesium	Cs	55	Neon	Ne	10	Thulium	Tm	69
Chlorine	Cl	17	Neptunium	Np	93	Tin	Sn	50
Chromium	Cr	24	Nickel	Ni	28	Titanium	Ti	22
Cobalt	Co	27	Niobium	Nb	41	Tungsten	W	74
Copper	Cu	29	Nitrogen	N	7	Uranium	U	92
Curium	Cm	96	Nobelium	No	102	Vanadium	V	23
Dysprosium	Dy	66	Osmium	Os	76	Xenon	Xe	54
Einsteinium	Es	99	Oxygen	O	8	Ytterbium	Yb	70
Erbium	Er	68	Palladium	Pd	46	Yttrium	Y	39
Europium	Eu	63	Phosphorus	P	15	Zinc	Zn	30
Fermium	Fm	100	Platinum	Pt	78	Zirconium	Zr	40
Fluorine	F	9	Plutonium	Pu	94			
Francium	Fr	87	Polonium	Po	84			
Gadolinium	Gd	64	Potassium	K	19			
Gallium	Ga	31	Praseodymium	Pr	59	(106)*		106
Germanium	Ge	32	Promethium	Pm	61	(107)		107
Gold	Au	79	Protactinium	Pa	91	(108)		108
Hafnium	Hf	72	Radium	Ra	88	(109)		109
Hahnium*	Ha	105	Radon	Rn	86			
Helium	He	2	Rhenium	Re	75			

* The official name and symbol have not been agreed upon.

Atomic Numbers

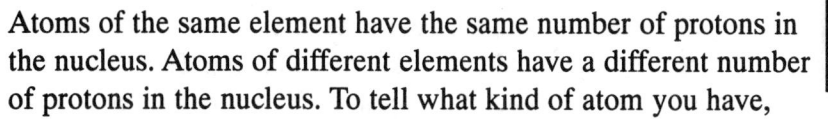

Atoms of the same element have the same number of protons in the nucleus. Atoms of different elements have a different number of protons in the nucleus. To tell what kind of atom you have, you need to know the number of protons in the nucleus of the atom. This is known as the *atomic number*. Atoms of an element may have a different number of neutrons in the nucleus. An atom with a different number of neutrons from other atoms of that element is called an *isotope*. The atomic number is given in a subscript that comes in front of the chemical symbol. The atomic number is not written in chemical equations because all atoms of the same element have the same number, but it is helpful in trying to identify an unknown element.

Use the chart on the previous page to help you find the atomic number of each of the following elements:

Carbon _____   Calcium _____   Oxygen _____

Often elements have a superscript, a number slightly higher than the chemical symbol that comes before the chemical symbol. This is the *mass number*, the total combined number of the protons plus the neutrons in the nucleus. The number of electrons in any atom is always the same as the number of protons, which means the net electrical charge of any atom is zero.

Use the chart on the previous page to help you answer the following questions:

1. What is the element with the chemical symbol Au? _____

   How many protons are in the nucleus of this atom? _____

   How many electrons are in one atom of Au? _____

2. What is the element with the chemical symbol C? _____

   How many protons are in the nucleus of this atom? _____

   How many electrons are in one atom of C? _____

The Periodic Table

1. The chart on the next page is the periodic table. Each box contains the chemical symbol for an element. The atomic number is written above the symbol. The periodic table is used for classifying or grouping the elements according to their common traits. If two elements have similar properties, they have a similar arrangement of electrons. The electrons of an atom orbit the nucleus in energy levels. An atom can have many different *energy levels*. The first and lowest level is the one closest to the nucleus. It can hold only two electrons. The second level can hold eight electrons and the third level can hold 32 electrons. The electrons usually come in pairs. If the level contains an odd number of electrons, it is a more unstable atom and is likely to lose or gain an electron. The periodic table is divided into 18 small groups of elements which belong to three larger categories—metal, nonmetal, and metalloid. Metals are often shiny and are good conductors of electricity and heat. They can usually be bent or pounded into thin sheets. Groups one through twelve are classified as *metals*. What metal from this group is used to make pennies?

   _____

2. Notice the dark zigzag lines on the table. The elements between these lines are *metalloids*. Metalloids have the characteristics of both metals and non-metals. What is the name of the very poisonous metalloid which is often used in rat poison?

   _____

3. *Nonmetals* tend to gain electrons. Group 17 is called the *halogens* from the Greek word for salt. NaCl is the chemical formula for table salt. What halogen(s) does table salt contain? _____

4. Group 18 is the nonmetal group called the *noble gases*. These elements are very stable and nonreactive. Which one of the noble gases is lighter than air and is often used to fill balloons? _____

5. Several of the other noble gases are used to fill glowing electric signs. Can you name one noble gas that is used for this purpose? _____

Periodic Table of the Elements

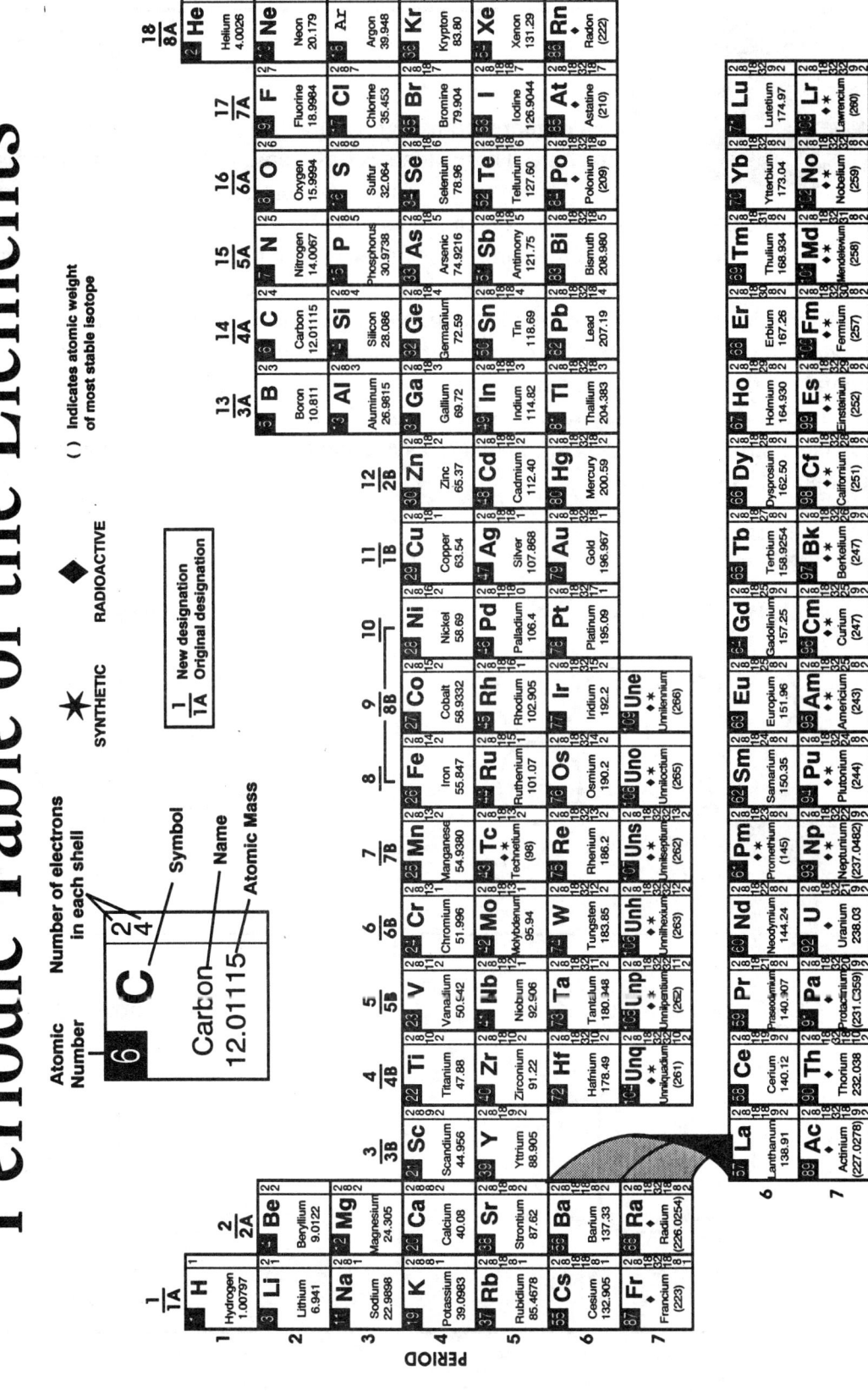

Molecules

Two or more atoms tightly attached to one another are a molecule. These atoms act as a unit, not as separate and distinct kinds of elements. Many elements exist as molecules naturally. Oxygen occurs naturally as two oxygen atoms linked together. The molecular formula of oxygen is written as O_2 and read aloud as "oh-two." The number two in the subscript that follows the chemical symbol shows that each molecule has two atoms. Any molecule that has two atoms is called a *diatomic molecule*. Ozone is another form of oxygen in which the molecules contain three atoms. Both pure oxygen and ozone contain nothing but oxygen, but they have very different chemical and physical properties. O_2 is necessary for animal life while O_3 is poisonous. O_2 has no odor while O_3 has a strong smell. Look at the diagrams and molecular formulas below. Label the compounds and the elements.

C_2H_4 Ethylene
or
C_6H_{12} Glucose

O_2

Oxygen

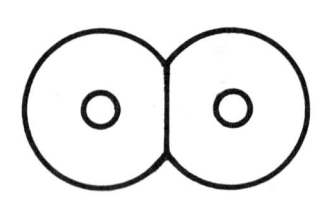

_____   _____

CO_2 Carbon dioxide

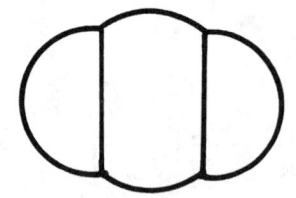

CO Carbon monoxide

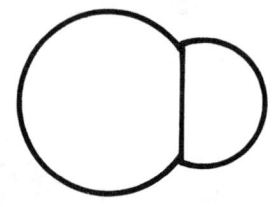

_____   _____

Ions

Using ordinary chemical processes, the nucleus of an atom remains unchanged, but the number of electrons in an atom can be changed easily. If electrons are removed from or added to an atom, the atom becomes electrically charged. This electrically charged atom is called an *ion*. A positively charged atom is called a *cation* (pronounced CATion). A negatively charged atom is called an *anion* (pronounced ANion).

To show that an atom has a positive charge, the superscript + is added after the chemical symbol. If the atom has lost only one electron, there is no number before the + sign. If the atom has lost two electrons, the superscript would be written 2+; if the atom has lost three electrons it would be 3+ and so on. For instance, Na+ is a sodium atom that has lost one electron.

To show that an atom has a negative charge, the superscript is added after the chemical symbol. If the atom has gained only one electron, there is no number before the sign. If the atom has gained two electrons, the superscript would be written 2-; if the atom has gained three electrons it would be 3- and so on. For example, Cl- is a chlorine atom with one extra electron.

Use The Periodic Table on page 13 to help you answer the questions below. Remember: the atomic weight = the number of protons in the nucleus.

1. What is the chemical symbol for the element with 13 protons and 10 electrons? _____
   What is the name of this element? _____

2. How many electrons does a Fe^{3+} atom have? _____
   How many protons does it have? _____
   What is the common name of this element? _____

3. How many electrons does an Se^{2-} atom have? _____
   How many protons does it have? _____
   What is the common name of this element? _____

What Is Special About Ions?

Some gases are very nonreactive chemically. Gases such as neon do not gain or lose electrons very readily. Outside of these gases, metal ions tend to be positively charged (cations) and nonmetals tend to be negatively charged (anions). When these metal and nonmetal ions combine to form a compound, it is called an *ionic compound.* Usually an ionic compound is composed of a nonmetal and a metal. An example of this is sodium chloride, which we know as table salt. Sodium chloride is a combination of the metal sodium and the nonmetal chlorine.

1. The sodium ion in sodium chloride has lost one electron. How do you write the chemical symbol for the sodium?

   _____

2. The chlorine ion in sodium chloride has one extra electron. How do you write the chemical symbol for the chlorine? _____

3. The sodium atoms and the chlorine atoms combine in equal numbers to form sodium chloride. How would you write the chemical formula for sodium chloride?

   _____

All chemical compounds are electrically neutral. If each atom of one ion has lost three electrons and each atom of the other ion has gained one electron, the elements in the compound must combine in a one to three ratio, with three of the negatively charged ion atoms for each atom of the positively charged ions. For example, Ba combines with Cl to give BaCl. This formula, BaCl, is called an *empirical formula.* An empirical formula shows the kinds of atoms and how many of each atom are in a molecule of that substance.

4. What is the empirical formula for Al^{3+} and Cl^{-}? _____

   What are the common names of the two elements in this compound? _____

The numbers in the superscripts have to balance. If one atom has lost three electrons (cation) and the other has gained only two electrons (anion), the empirical formula must contain two of the cations and three of the anions to balance.

5. What is the empirical formula for Al^{3+} and O^{2-}? _____

Organic Compounds

In the 1700s, scientists developed the "vitalist theory," which stated that organic compounds came from living organisms. In 1828, a German chemist named Friedrich Wohler mixed potassium cyanate (KOCN), with ammonium chloride (NH_4Cl) and produced urea (H_2NCONH_2). Urea comes naturally from the urine of animals. Today, many organic compounds are produced from inorganic materials. The modern definition of an organic compound is not just a compound that comes from a living organism, but any compound that contains carbon as the main element. Since more than seven million carbon-based compounds have already been identified and more are being discovered each year, the study of organic compounds has become a separate branch of chemistry.

Look at the chemical formulas below. Place an "O" beside the organic compounds and an "I" beside the inorganic compounds.

1. _____ $C_6H_{12}O_6$ glucose

2. _____ H_2O water

3. _____ H_2O_2 hydrogen peroxide

4. _____ C_3H_8 propane

5. _____ $C_{12}H_{22}O_{11}$ table sugar

6. Which of the compounds above can normally be found in living organisms?
   _____
   _____

7. One group of organic compounds is called *hydrocarbons* because they are composed exclusively of hydrogen and carbon. Look at the compounds below. What are they? What do they have in common? _____
   _____

    CH_4 = Methane C_3H_6 = Propane C_3H_8 = Butane

Chemical Equations

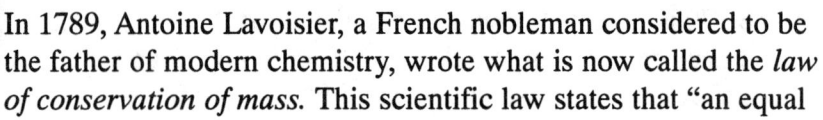

In 1789, Antoine Lavoisier, a French nobleman considered to be the father of modern chemistry, wrote what is now called the *law of conservation of mass*. This scientific law states that "an equal amount of matter exists both before and after the experiment." In other words, in any *chemical reaction,* matter is neither created nor destroyed. A chemical reaction is simply the process by which two or more substances are converted into a third substance. For example, the process of creating water (H_2O) from hydrogen and oxygen is a chemical reaction. To show this chemical reaction, we write a *chemical equation.* The chemical equation for making water from hydrogen and oxygen is written this way:

$$2H_2 + O_2 \longrightarrow 2H_2O$$

The + sign means "reacts with" or "combines with" and the arrow means "produces." In other words, this equation says that two hydrogen molecules combine with one oxygen molecule to make two molecules of water. The large number before each chemical symbol indicates the number of molecules of the element or compound. Remember that the subscript indicates how many atoms are in one molecule of the element. Both oxygen and hydrogen are diatonic molecules. The equation above shows that there are four atoms of hydrogen and two atoms of oxygen on each side of the arrow. This means that the equations are balanced. A chemical equation cannot have any fractions in it. What numbers and chemical symbols do you need to add to balance the equations below?

1. _____ Al + _____ HCl $\longrightarrow$ 2 $AlCl_3$ + 3H_2
2. CH_4 + 2O_2 $\longrightarrow$ CO_2 + _____ H_2O

To show the physical state of the elements in an equation or to indicate whether the element is dissolved in water, the symbols (g) for gas, (l) for liquid, (s) for solid, and (aq) for aqueous follow the element or compound. Complete the following equations:

3. _____ $K_{(s)}$ + _____ $H_2O_{(l)}$ $\longrightarrow$ 2$KOH_{(g)}$ + $H_{2(g)}$

4. What are the physical states of the chemicals which are combined in the equation above? _____

5. _____ $Na_{(s)}$ + _____ $H_2O_{(l)}$ $\longrightarrow$ 2$NaOH_{(aq)}$ + $H_{2(g)}$

Solutions

A solution is a mixture of atoms that is uniform or the same throughout the mixture. An example of a mixture is sugar or $C_{12}H_{22}O_{11}$ dissolved in water. Using a clean glass and a clean spoon, stir a teaspoon of sugar into a large glass of clean water until all of the sugar is dissolved and no grains of sugar are visible at the bottom of the glass. Taste a spoonful of sugar water from the top of the glass. Pour the top half of the sugar water into a second clean glass. Taste a spoonful of sugar water from the top of what remains in the first glass. Is there a difference in taste? _____

_____

A solution is not necessarily simply a solid dissolved in a liquid. Air is a solution. Steel is a solid solution of iron combined with carbon. Which of the following items are solutions? Mark an "S" before each solution.

_____ 1. Pepsi

_____ 2. seawater

_____ 3. an oil slick on the ocean

_____ 4. a chocolate chip cookie

_____ 5. a glass of Kool-aid

If a solid is dissolved in water, the solution is called *aqueous*. The water is called the *solvent* and the solid is called the *solute*.

6. In the case of the sugar water, which item is the solvent? _____

7. Which item is the solute? _____

8. Can you name some other aqueous solutions? _____

If the solvent is alcohol, the solution is called a *tincture*. The iodine you find in your medicine cabinet is a tincture. The element iodine is dissolved in alcohol to make a liquid which you can use to cleanse a small wound and help it to heal.

Electrolytes

Some solutions conduct electricity better than others. Solutions which are good electrical conductors are called *electrolytes*. Electrolytes contain *ions*. Sodium chloride or salt in water is a good electrolyte. Na^+ and Cl^- are dispersed or spread through the water when the salt dissolves. Some substances do not form ions when they are dissolved in water. Sugar is one of these substances. Sugar is called a *nonelectrolyte*.

1. Electrolytes are particularly useful in the process of electroplating or coating items with a thin layer of metal and in making batteries. *Dry cell* batteries contain a paste of ammonium chloride and a solution of manganese dioxide. The diagram to the right shows how the battery is made. Are ammonium chloride and manganese dioxide electrolytes or nonelectrolytes? _____

2. What are some items which are electroplated? What metals are used to cover these items? _____
_____

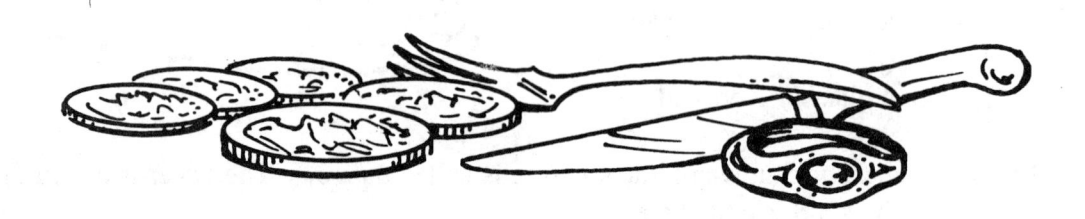

Electrolytes are responsible for the "hardness" or "softness" of your tap water. Hard water contains many ions, especially iron (Fe^{2+} or Fe^{3+}) and calcium (Ca^{2+}) ions. These ions combine with the fatty acids in soap to form a crusty deposit. The water can be "softened" and the ions removed by using a water softener which removes the ions from the water.

3. Would hard water or plain water be a better conductor of electricity? _____
_____

Concentrations

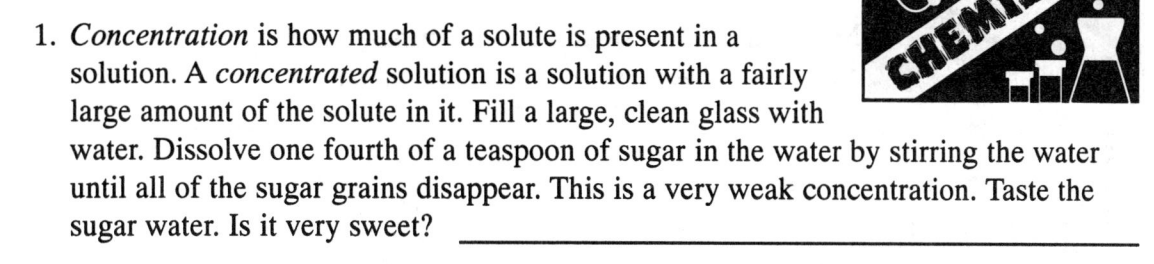

1. *Concentration* is how much of a solute is present in a solution. A *concentrated* solution is a solution with a fairly large amount of the solute in it. Fill a large, clean glass with water. Dissolve one fourth of a teaspoon of sugar in the water by stirring the water until all of the sugar grains disappear. This is a very weak concentration. Taste the sugar water. Is it very sweet? _____

2. Now stir more sugar into the water a teaspoonful at a time, stirring until all of the sugar is dissolved. Do not add more sugar until all of the sugar in the water is dissolved. Stop when you have grains of sugar at the bottom of the glass and you cannot get them to dissolve. Taste the water. This is a *saturated* solution. The water is holding as much dissolved sugar as possible. Taste the water. How is this sugar water different from the first taste? _____

3. Fill one clean, empty glass with cold water. Add two ice cubes to the water and stir until the water is very cold. Fill a second clean, empty glass with hot tap water. Add sugar one teaspoonful at a time to each glass, stirring each time until the sugar is completely dissolved. Stop adding sugar when there are grains of sugar at the bottom of the glass which will not dissolve. Which glass of water holds more dissolved sugar? _____

4. If you wanted to dissolve more of a solute in water, what could you do to the water to make the solute dissolve more easily?

_____

_____

Making Crystals

Materials: Three small, shallow dishes, warm water, salt, sugar, alum, and a stainless steel or plastic spoon

Procedure:
1. Fill each dish with one half inch of warm water. Label the first dish "salt," the second dish "sugar," and the third dish "alum." Dissolve as much salt as possible in the water in the first dish, dissolve as much sugar as possible in the second dish, and as much alum as possible in the third dish.

2. Place the three dishes in a sunny warm location. Observe the dishes every three days. What happens?

_____
_____

3. What you see in the dishes when all of the water evaporates is crystals. Are all of the crystals the same shape? _____

Draw what you see in the spaces below:

SALT   **SUGAR**   **ALUM**

Chemical Reactions

1. Chemical reactions are classified as either *ectothermic* or *endothermic*. In ectothermic reactions, heat is produced or passes from the reaction to its surroundings. In endothermic reactions, heat is absorbed from the surroundings. If you touched a test tube which contained an endothermic reaction, how would the test tube feel? _____

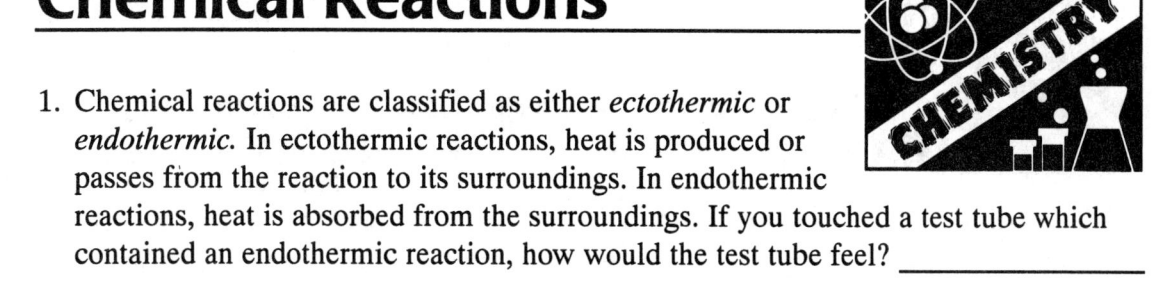

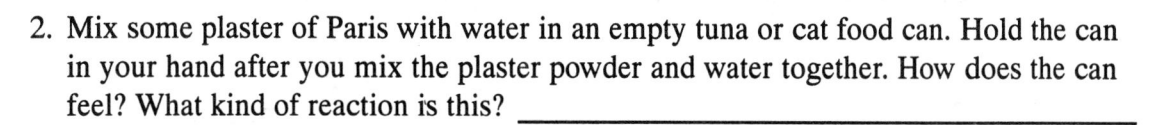

2. Mix some plaster of Paris with water in an empty tuna or cat food can. Hold the can in your hand after you mix the plaster powder and water together. How does the can feel? What kind of reaction is this? _____

3. A combustion reaction is a reaction which burns or produces a flame. Most combustion reactions are the result of O_2 from the air reacting with a substance. For example, when heat is applied to propane (C_3H_8), the oxygen in the air combines with the propane to produce carbon dioxide and water. This reaction also produces a large amount of heat. The chemical equation for this reaction is shown below. Balance the equation.

   $$C_3H_{8\,(g)} + 5O_{2\,(g)} \longrightarrow \underline{} CO_{2\,(g)} + \underline{} H_2O_{(l)}$$

4. In what state(s) are the propane and the oxygen which are combined in the reaction? _____

5. In what state(s) are the carbon dioxide and the water which are produced by this reaction? _____

6. Look at the pictures and read the descriptions below. Label the reactions *ectothermic* or *endothermic*. _____

A. _____   B. _____

The flame touches the hydrogen-filled balloon. The balloon bursts into flame.

This paint stripper is applied to a painted board. The paint bubbles and feels cold to the touch.

Catalysts

The rate at which chemicals react can often be increased by adding a *catalyst*. The catalyst controls the rate of the reaction. Sometimes the catalyst remains separate from the chemicals which are being combined, and sometimes the catalyst is also changed in the reaction. The enzymes in your saliva which break foods down into simple sugars are an example of catalysts. The enzymes themselves do not nourish your body or become part of the digested food.

1. To see an enzyme at work, fill a clean, glass jar three-fourths full with hydrogen peroxide. (You can buy this at a pharmacy.) Place a small piece of uncooked calves' liver in the liquid and place the jar lid on top of the jar but do not fasten it. What happens? _____

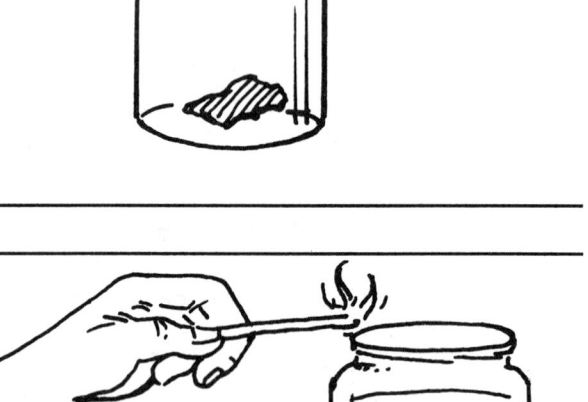

_____

2. Light a wooden safety match or a splint of wood and blow it out. Quickly remove the cap of the jar and insert the still-warm match tip into the air space at the top of the jar. What happens? _____

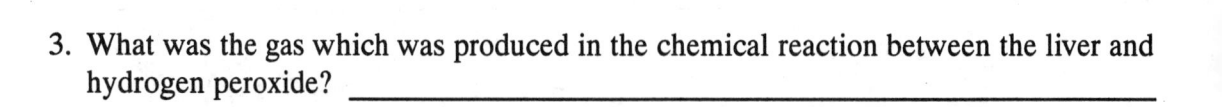

_____

3. What was the gas which was produced in the chemical reaction between the liver and hydrogen peroxide? _____

_____

Catalysts are also used in catalytic converters, the devices which help to reduce air pollution from cars. Catalytic converters help the engine burn fuel more efficiently, thus producing less waste and pollution.

Qualitative Analysis

Qualitative analysis is the process of analyzing a substance to find out what is in it. This is particularly useful for detectives, pharmacists, and doctors as well as scientists. Food is analyzed for vitamin content and separate ingredients, gasoline is analyzed for octane levels, and unknown substances are tested simply to identify them. To perform qualitative analysis on a lab sample, you need an *indicator*. An indicator is a liquid or other substance which reacts a certain way with already identified substances. For instance, iodine turns dark purple-blue when it comes in contact with anything that contains starch. Iodine is an indicator for starch.

1. Test this fact for yourself. Take small samples of potato, bread, cheese, orange juice (one teaspoonful of a liquid in a saucer is sufficient), apple juice, milk, banana, and a piece of Kleenex or toilet tissue. Drop one drop of tincture of iodine (obtainable from a pharmacy) on each item. Which items are starches? _____

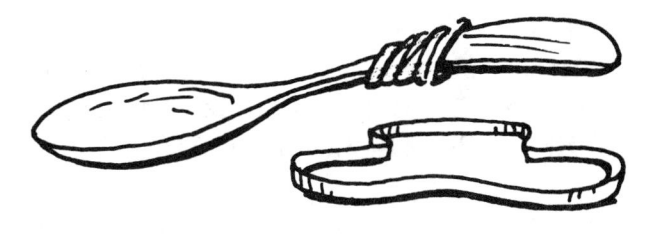

2. Silver tarnishes or turns dark when it comes in contact with sulfur. Wrap a rubber band around a silver teaspoon. Leave the rubber band on for five days. What happens to the teaspoon? _____

3. Place the bowl of the silver teaspoon in a raw egg for one hour. What happens? Does egg contain sulfur? _____

4. How could you test to see if something was made of silver? _____

Acids

Acids are electrolytes which are able to donate a hydrogen ion when they are dissolved in water. This increases the concentration of H_2. Since a hydrogen ion contains just one proton and one electron, a hydrogen ion is just a single proton with no electron. For this reason, acids are also called *proton donors*.

Many common substances are acids. Vinegar is acetic acid. Vitamin C is ascorbic acid. To test for acids, you need an acid indicator. One indicator is litmus paper. Litmus paper turns pink when it comes in contact with an acid. Turmeric (a spice you can find in the grocery store), phenolphthalein (an ingredient in ExLax), and red cabbage are also good indicators. To make these indicators, purchase each of the items and follow the directions below.

1. Mix a teaspoonful of turmeric in one-fourth cup of rubbing alcohol. Pour it into a clean glass or jar. Label it TURMERIC INDICATOR. **(DO NOT DRINK THIS.)**

2. Chop one cup of red cabbage into small bits and place it in a saucepan. Cover the cabbage with water and **WITH ADULT SUPERVISION**, boil it for five minutes. Let it cool. Pour the red liquid into a clean glass or jar. This liquid is the indicator. Label it RED CABBAGE INDICATOR.

3. Crush the ExLax tablet in a small saucer. Cover the crushed tablet with rubbing alcohol and stir until it is dissolved. Set the mixture aside and let it settle. Use a medicine dropper to transfer the clear liquid to a clean jar or glass. Label it PHENOLPHTHALEIN INDICATOR.

4. Cut a white paper towel or heavy white art paper in one-inch strips. Soak five strips in each indicator. Let the strips dry and label the strips with the name of the indicator you used.

5. Dip the unlabeled end of the indicator strips you made in step four in vinegar. What color do they turn in the presence of an acid?
   Turmeric indicator: _____
   Red cabbage indicator: _____
   Phenolphthalein indicator: _____

Bases

Bases are also electrolytes. They react with or accept hydrogen ions. Where an acid increases the concentration of hydrogen ions in water, a base increases the concentration of hydroxide or OH ions in water. If the acid and the base are put together, the two ions unite to form water. Soap is a strong base.

1. You can use the indicators you have made to test for bases as well as acids. Take the second of each kind of indicator strip and test it in a saucer of liquid hand soap. What colors do the indicators turn when they come in contact with a base?

   Litmus paper: _____

   Turmeric indicator: _____

   Red cabbage indicator: _____

   Phenolphthalein indicator: _____

2. Now test some other substances, such as milk of magnesia, soft drinks, tea, egg white, baking soda (mixed with water), fruit juice, and Maalox or Rolaids (dissolved in water). Place one tablespoonful of each item in clean saucers and dip the unlabeled end of the fresh indicators in them. What are the results? List the items being tested, the indicators, and the results on the chart below.

ITEM	INDICATOR	RESULTS

3. What happens if you dip the indicator in vinegar and then immediately dip it in liquid soap? _____

4. How can you change the colors of the indicators back to their original color?
   _____
   _____

5. What happens if you dip the indicators in water? _____
   _____

Precipitates

1. Fill a glass or glass jar half full with hot tap water. Stir one teaspoonful of alum (look in the grocery store under pickling supplies) into the water until it is completely dissolved. Add two teaspoons of ammonia. What happens?

_____
_____

What you see is a *precipitate*. It is a solid substance which "drops out" of a solution after a chemical reaction. This precipitate is *insoluble*; it cannot be dissolved in water.

2. Measure four tablespoonfuls of vinegar into a second clean glass or glass jar. Drop one Tums tablet into the vinegar. What happens? (Use both your eyes and your ears to observe this reaction.)

_____
_____

3. Set the glass aside for one hour. Observe the result. What has happened? What do you have in the glass? _____
_____

4. Antacids are bases. Different antacids contain different elements, but all neutralize the effect of acids. The stomach contains hydrochloric acid. The Tums neutralizes the effect of the acid and leaves a calcium deposit in the stomach which may be digested. Test other antacids in vinegar. Do they all do the same thing? Do they all produce precipitates? _____
_____

© Instructional Fair • TS Denison   IF2716 Physical Science

Isotopes

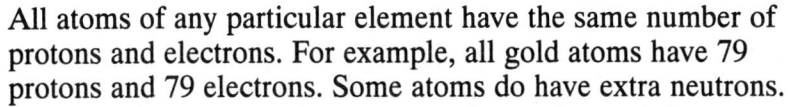

All atoms of any particular element have the same number of protons and electrons. For example, all gold atoms have 79 protons and 79 electrons. Some atoms do have extra neutrons. This means they keep the same atomic number and the same electrical charge, but they have a greater mass. These atoms with the extra neutrons are called *isotopes*. Sometimes these isotopes are unstable and "decay" into another isotope or even element. This occurs when the unstable isotope loses an *alpha-particle* which consists of two protons and two electrons. The decay of an isotope takes a set amount of time for each element. Some elements decay at a rate of a few seconds and some decay at a rate of millions of years. The decay rate is known as the *half-life*.

Carbon-14 ($^{14}_{6}$C) has a half-life of 5,730 years.

Carbon-14 *dating* uses this information to date the remains of objects made of organic compounds such as wood, parchment, natural fibers, and bones. Living organisms have a constant amount of carbon-14. When the organism dies, no more carbon-14 enters the organism and the carbon-14 that is present starts to decay. Scientists can tell how old the item is by the amount of carbon-14 that remains.

Neutrons and protons are the heavy part of an atom. To find out how many neutrons and how many protons are in any given isotope, you subtract the *atomic number* from the *atomic weight*. The atomic weight is the number given in the *superscript* that precedes the chemical symbol (the higher number that comes before the chemical symbol). The *atomic weight* is the *subscript* or lower number that precedes the chemical symbol. An atom of an isotope is called a *nuclide*. Give the number of protons and the number of neutrons in each of the nuclides below.

1. $^{37}_{17}$Cl _____

2. $^{197}_{79}$Au _____

3. $^{39}_{19}$K _____

4. $^{40}_{18}$Ar _____

Force

Force is the push or pull that one object exerts on another. If you push a book across the table, the power that you use to push that book is force. If you pull a shade down on a window, the power that you use is force. Force can affect an object in one of three ways. Force can start the object moving or stop the object from moving. Force can cause the object to move in a different direction. Force can change the speed of the object's movement. Read the examples below. What is the force doing to the object in each case?

1. A soccer ball rolling toward the goal is kicked back to the center of the field.

2. The referee throws a basketball up in the air for a jump shot. _____

3. The shortstop catches the fly ball. _____

4. The bike rider pedals faster, causing the bicycle to speed up. _____

5. Objects do not have to touch each other to exert force. One kind of force pulls objects to the earth. Do you know what it is? What force makes your pencil fall to the floor if you let it go? _____

6. *Centrifugal* force is the force which tends to make a rotating object fly away from the center of rotation. Tie a piece of thread to a small bead. Hold the other end of the string and swing the bead in a circle. The force that pulls the string taut and keeps the bead flying in a circle parallel to the floor is centrifugal force.

Magnetism

Materials: Two bar magnets (or two pieces, each two inches long, cut from a small roll of magnetic tape), a round magnet, a horseshoe magnet, string, scissors, iron filings (or small bits of steel wool), a compass, and two sheets of white drawing paper

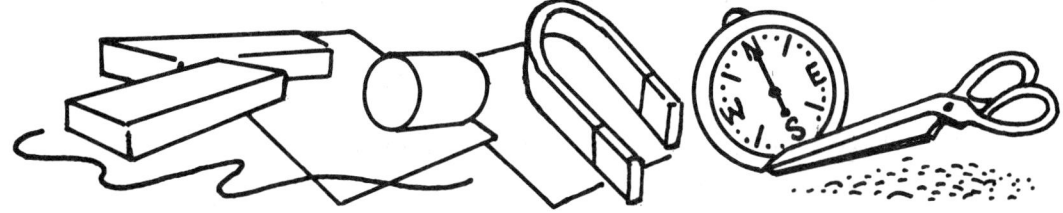

Procedure:

1. Tie a piece of string around one bar magnet. Suspend the magnet in the air. Does it point a certain way? What happens if you turn the magnet the other way? _____

2. Place the magnet next to the compass. What happens? _____

3. Turn the magnet around so it points the other way. What happens to the compass?

4. The magnet and the compass both have *poles*. The earth is a giant magnet and it also has poles. These are the parts of the magnets (or the earth) where the magnetic force is the strongest. The compass needle is a magnet, and it points to the north pole of the earth. In magnets, opposites attract each other and like poles repel. For this reason, the compass needle moves away from the like pole of your magnet and moves toward the opposite pole. What pole of the compass needle is actually pointing to the north pole of the earth? _____

5. Place one bar magnet under the piece of drawing paper. Sprinkle the iron filings on the paper over the magnet. Draw the pattern you see on the second sheet of art paper.

6. What you observe in the pattern that you drew are the *magnetic field lines* of your magnet. If you have a horseshoe magnet or a round magnet, repeat step 5. Do you have a different pattern? _____

7. What kind of metal is attracted to magnets? Is any other element attracted to magnets

Electromagnets

An electromagnet is a magnet made from a coil of wire with an electric current running through it. The flow of electrons gives the coil a north and a south pole and makes it a magnet. This kind of magnet can be made very large and very strong, but it is temporary. When the electric current is turned off, the magnetism is gone. What could a magnet like this be used for? _____

_____

Materials: A large iron (steel) nail, one meter of bell wire, paper clips, scissors, electrical tape, a compass, and a D-battery

Procedure:
1. Use the scissors to remove the one inch of coating from both ends of the wire.

2. Wrap the wire tightly around the nail, making the coils as close as possible.

3. Tape one end of the wire to one battery terminal. Tape the other end of the wire to the other battery terminal.

4. Bring the compass near the nail. What happens? _____

_____

5. Place the compass beside the nail. Undo the electrical tape and turn the battery around so the wire ends are taped to the opposite terminals.
   What happens? _____

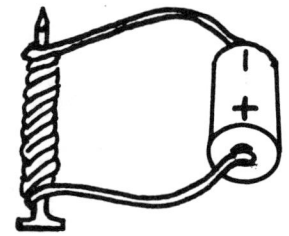

_____

6. The electricity flowing through the wire has turned the nail into what? _____

7. Disconnect the wires from the battery. Is the nail still a magnet? _____

© Instructional Fair • TS Denison   32   IF2716 Physical Science

Other Kinds of Force

1. Gravity, centrifugal force, and magnetism are not the only kinds of force. *Friction* is another kind of force. Rub your hands together. Do they get warmer? The force that makes them warmer is friction. What else can friction do? What happens if you walk on a slippery, wet floor? The water on the floor reduces the friction. This is what the world would be like without the force of friction. What does friction do? _____

2. Does friction make things move more easily or does it oppose motion? _____

3. *Electricity* is a force. This force is closely related to magnetism. Electrically charged particles attract and repel each other just like the poles on a magnet. Break a piece of a Styrofoam cup or Styrofoam packing material into several small pieces. Inflate a balloon and rub it against your hair. Place the balloon near the Styrofoam pieces. What happens? _____

4. Place the balloon near a piece of your hair. What happens? _____

5. The Styrofoam has a negative charge. What kind of charge does the balloon have?
_____

6. *Nuclear* force is another important and very strong force. The bonds between the particles in the nucleus of an atom release incredibly large amounts of energy when they are broken.

7. Another force is *centripetal* force. This is the force required to hold a revolving object in a circular path. Centrifugal force makes the bead on the string pull away from the center of rotation. To keep the bead on the string and going in a circle requires a certain amount of force. This is centripetal force.

Are Forces Always Balanced?

If a force acting on an object has an equal but opposite force opposing it, we say that the forces are *balanced*. If one hockey player pushes the puck to the right and a player from the other team pushes the puck left until it is back in its original position, those forces are balanced. For example, if you sit on the ground, your weight is a force pushing downward. The ground is exerting an equal but opposite force upward, so you do not move. If the ground exerted less force upward, you would sink as if you were in quicksand or water. If the ground exerted more force, you would rise.

1. If the forces are not balanced, if they are unequal, there is a *net force* or the amount of extra force that is pushing in one direction. For example, once a rocket breaks free of the earth's gravity, it continues to move straight ahead. The force of gravity holds things in place on earth and pulls loose objects back to the earth. What happens in outer space where there is no gravity to act on loose things? _____

2. Jupiter's gravitational force is 2.5 times that of earth. That means a person can jump 2.5 times higher on earth than on Jupiter. If a person can jump 2.5 feet on earth, how high can he/she jump on Jupiter? _____

3. On the moon you can jump six times as high as you can jump on earth. What does this tell you about the moon's gravitational force? _____

4. Would it take more force to launch a rocket on the moon or on Jupiter? Why? _____

The Laws of Motion

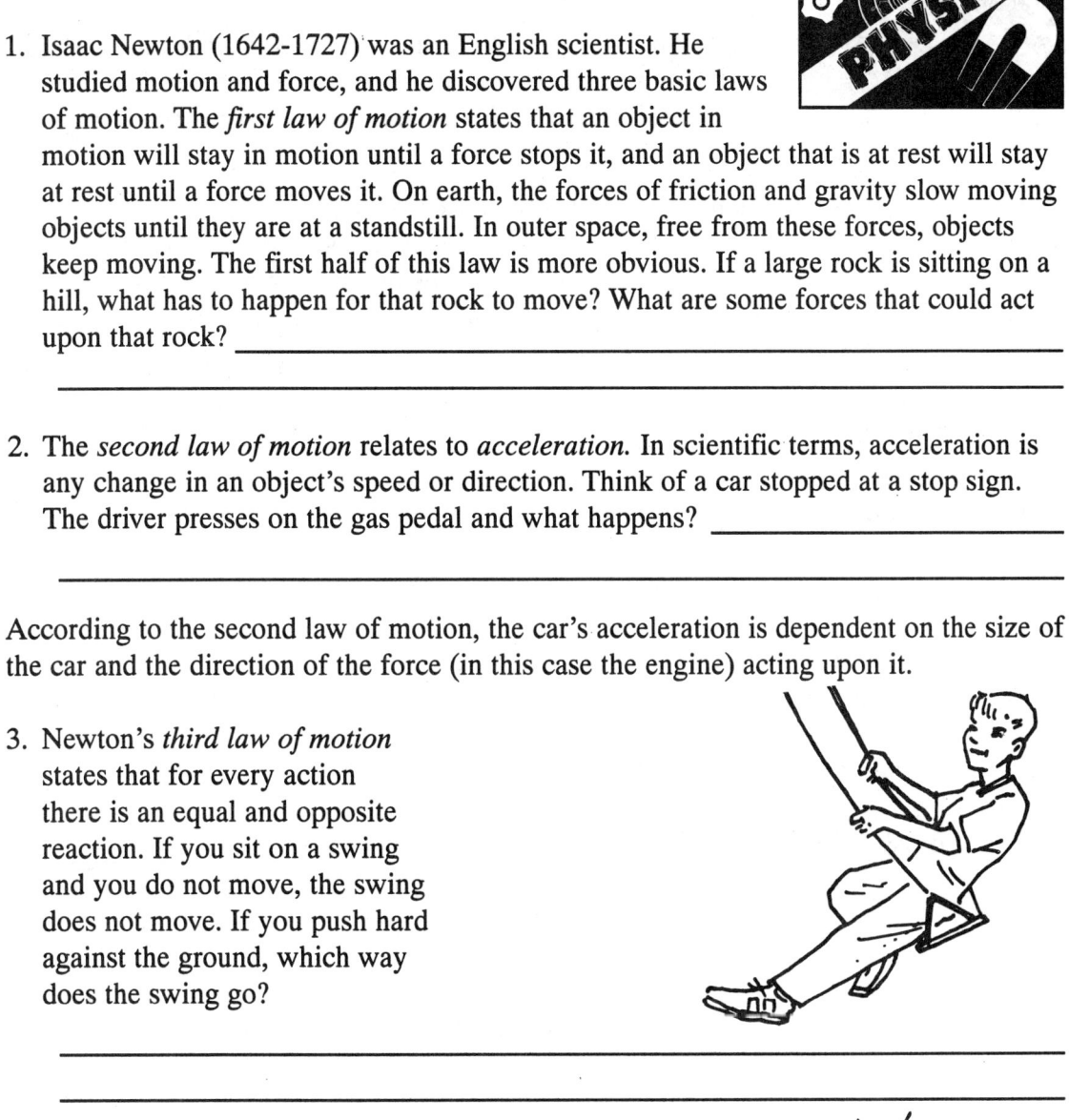

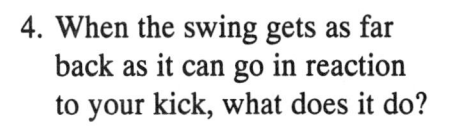

1. Isaac Newton (1642-1727) was an English scientist. He studied motion and force, and he discovered three basic laws of motion. The *first law of motion* states that an object in motion will stay in motion until a force stops it, and an object that is at rest will stay at rest until a force moves it. On earth, the forces of friction and gravity slow moving objects until they are at a standstill. In outer space, free from these forces, objects keep moving. The first half of this law is more obvious. If a large rock is sitting on a hill, what has to happen for that rock to move? What are some forces that could act upon that rock? _____

    _____

2. The *second law of motion* relates to *acceleration*. In scientific terms, acceleration is any change in an object's speed or direction. Think of a car stopped at a stop sign. The driver presses on the gas pedal and what happens? _____

    _____

According to the second law of motion, the car's acceleration is dependent on the size of the car and the direction of the force (in this case the engine) acting upon it.

3. Newton's *third law of motion* states that for every action there is an equal and opposite reaction. If you sit on a swing and you do not move, the swing does not move. If you push hard against the ground, which way does the swing go?

    _____

    _____

4. When the swing gets as far back as it can go in reaction to your kick, what does it do?

    _____

    _____

Motion

Motion is the changing of position. *Position* is the location or place where an object is in relation to a given reference point. For instance, if the chair is two feet from the table, that is the position of the chair.

Everything in the universe is moving. A chair on a floor in a classroom on earth is constantly moving because the planet is revolving around the sun. If you compare the chair to the sun, the chair is constantly changing its position. It is moving. If you compare the chair to the table sitting on the floor in the classroom, the chair is not moving.

Speed and velocity are two ways we measure motion. *Speed* is a measurement of how far an object moves in a given period of time. You can use a speedometer to find out the speed of a vehicle at any given time. You use an equation to find out the average speed of an object or animal over a period of time:

$$\text{Average Speed} = \frac{\text{total distance}}{\text{total time}}$$

You state the answer in miles or kilometers per hour (m/h or km/h) or miles per second or kilometers per second (m/s or km/s).

1. If a runner runs a 10-kilometer race in 2.3 hours, what is his average speed? _____

2. If a car drives a 200-mile race in 1.25 hours, what is its average speed? _____

3. Velocity is what is called a *vector quantity*. A vector quantity is anything that describes both the amount and the direction of the force. Velocity describes both the direction and the speed of the object. It is often written with an arrow to show that it indicates direction. Meteorologists often use the term velocity to describe something. Do you know what that something is? _____

If we are describing the velocity of an object, such as a bus, we describe it in terms of km/h or m/h still, but we also include the direction. If two buses are traveling at forty miles per hour, but one is traveling east and one is traveling west, they are traveling at the same speed but at different velocities. If they are traveling in the same direction, they are traveling at the same velocity.

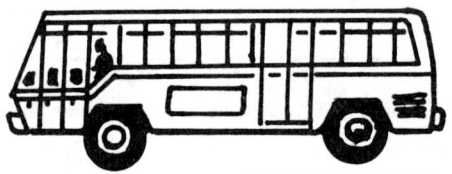

The Theory of Relativity

Newton's laws of motion apply in most situations, but when those laws are applied to subatomic particles or distant parts of the universe, they do not seem to work. Albert Einstein (1879-1955), the German-born American physicist, developed the theory of relativity. The theory of relativity comes from the idea that absolute speeds cannot be measured. All speeds are measured in relation to something that is known. This is because everything in the universe is moving. Do you remember the chair on the floor? That chair is not moving if you compare it to the desk on the floor next to it, but it is moving if you compare it to the sun. The sun is also moving in our galaxy, the Milky Way.

The second fact that Einstein used was the speed of light—186,291 miles per second. From these two facts, he reasoned that no material object can travel at a speed greater than the speed of light. As an object approaches the speed of light, it increases in mass. If it actually reached the speed of light, its mass would become infinite. An infinite mass would need an infinite force to propel it. In addition, as the velocity of an object increases in relation to a viewer, its length decreases—it shrinks. A third interesting conclusion is that time for a moving object is shorter. That may mean that we could travel for years in space at speeds at or near the speed of light and find that we had been away only a few months in earth time.

1. What do you think? Is it possible to travel at or beyond the speed of light? _____

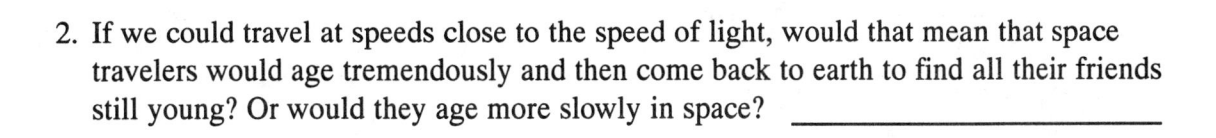

_____

2. If we could travel at speeds close to the speed of light, would that mean that space travelers would age tremendously and then come back to earth to find all their friends still young? Or would they age more slowly in space? _____

_____

Einstein's famous equation $E = mc^2$ was developed to show the relationship between mass and energy. E is energy, m is mass, and c is the speed of light. This explains the behavior of the atoms in an atomic bomb, for example. When the atoms split (fission) or bond together (fusion), a small amount of mass is lost. This mass is released as energy.

Work

1. The scientific definition of *work* is very specific. When a force moves an object, *work* is done. Nothing else is work. Studying science is not work by this definition. Moving the pages of the textbook is work. Pushing against a wall that does not move is not work, no matter how hard you push. If the wall does not move, it is not work. Which of the pictures below shows work being done? _____

2. By scientific definition, the amount of work done depends on how much force was applied to the object and how far the object moved. If you lift a weight over your head, you have done more work than if you just lift the weight to your shoulder. Which picture below shows more work? _____

3. Now look at these pictures. Which one shows more work being done? _____
Why? _____

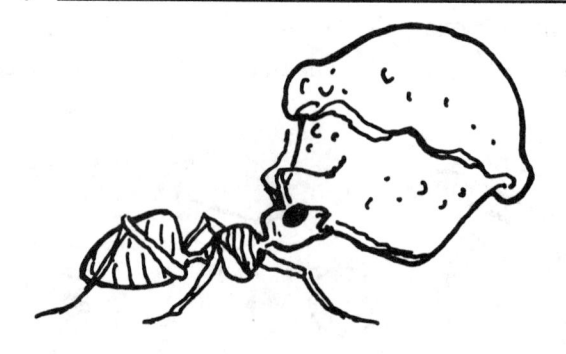

Simple Machines

A *simple machine* is something that changes the direction of the force or the amount of force required to move an object. A *compound machine* is made of two or more simple machines. The illustrations and descriptions on this page show the four simple machines. One example of these simple machines is already given. Can you give one more example of each of these simple machines?

1. LEVER—The lever is a pole or board resting on a rock or other object (this is called the *fulcrum*). The force is applied to one end and this lifts the object on the other end. 
   Another example: _____

2. INCLINED PLANE—The inclined plane is a ramp or anything that looks like a ramp. It is easier to walk up (or push something else up) or slide down an inclined plane. 
   Another example: _____

3. WHEELS AND AXLES—Almost every wheel or wheel-shaped thing you can think of is an example of a wheel and axle. The doorknob, for instance, is a wheel and axle. The axle is the pole or shaft that holds the wheel in place. 
   Another example: _____

4. PULLEY—Pulleys are found on clotheslines that can be reeled in. The pulley looks like a wheel with a rope or string wrapped around it.

   Another example (hint: reread the first sentence after the word PULLEY. One word in that sentence may remind you of an example of a pulley.

Using Simple Machines

We often think of simple machines as tools, not machines. We use a screwdriver without realizing it is a lever. No one thinks of a doorknob as a wheel and axle. We also do not think of the force needed to make these machines work. That force is called *effort*. The machine is also exerting a force on the object. The force exerted by the machine is called *resistance*. The machine exerts resistance at the point where the machine contacts the object. This is most obvious in the lever. With a lever, you can apply the force at different points. The distance between the effort and the object and the placement of the *fulcrum* can greatly affect how much work can be done.

Materials: A ruler, a fist-sized rock, and several paperback books

Procedure:

1. Place the ruler on top of the rock like a seesaw, with an equal amount of ruler on either side of the rock. Stack the paperback books on one side of the ruler. How many books can you lift using just one finger?

   _____

2. Move the ruler so the longest part of the ruler is on the book side of the rock. How many books can you lift with one finger now?

   _____

3. Move the ruler so the longest part of the ruler is on the side of the rock near your hand. How many books can you lift with one finger now?

   _____

4. How can you move a lever to make lifting a load easier?

   _____

Can a Machine Be More Efficient?

Efficient means to be more competent, less wasteful, and in a machine it means that the machine will run better. One of the main problems that reduces the efficiency of a machine is *friction*. The force that helps us keep a grip on a smooth surface and keeps our tires from skidding on the road causes overheating and wear and tear on machine parts that grind and rub against each other constantly. There are several solutions to the problem, but none of these solutions completely eliminate the problem.

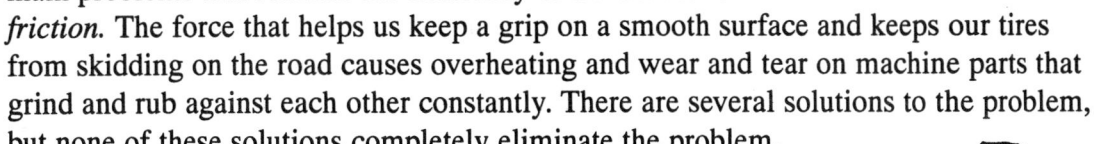

1. To increase efficiency and decrease friction, you can add a *lubricant.* Rub your fingers together. Now grease your fingers with cooking oil. Rub your fingers together again. What happens? Did the oil reduce the friction between your fingers? _____

    What is one example of a lubricant? _____

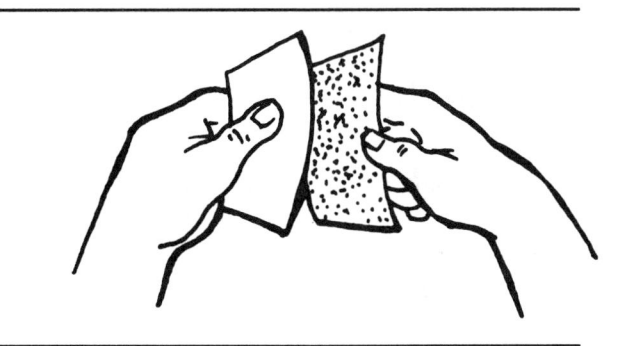

2. You can make the surfaces smoother to reduce the friction. Rub two pieces of coarse sandpaper together (rough, sandy sides against each other). Next, rub two pieces of smooth typing paper together. Which is easier? _____

3. Round, smooth *ball bearings* reduce friction. Tie a piece of string around a large book. Pull the string to move the book. Next, place ten marbles on the floor under the book. Pull the string to move the book a second time.
    Which is easier? _____

© Instructional Fair • TS Denison
IF2716 Physical Science

Energy

In scientific terms, *energy* is the ability to do work. Energy exerts the force on the object. You cannot see the energy, but you can see the effects it produces. This energy is always classified as either *kinetic* or *potential*. Kinetic energy is moving energy. A dog running after a ball is demonstrating kinetic energy. Potential energy is energy at rest. It is the ability to do work, energy waiting to be used. A cat crouched behind a mouse displays potential energy. This changes into kinetic energy when the cat pounces. (Kinetic energy changes to potential energy when a force causes the object to change position.) Read the descriptions and look at the pictures below. Label each item kinetic or potential depending on which kind of energy is displayed.

1. The track star runs toward the finish line.

2. The rock teeters on the edge of the cliff.

3. The car is parked with the key in the ignition.

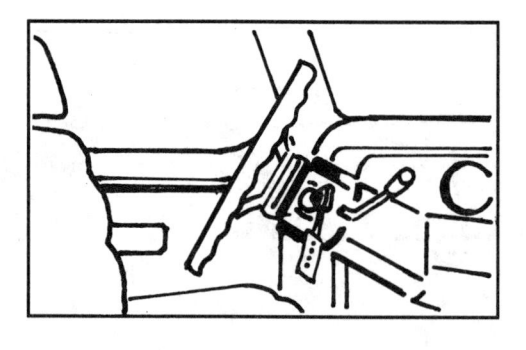

4. The water flows down the cliff.

Different Forms of Energy

1. There are many different forms or kinds of energy. *Mechanical energy* is the energy of motion. Things that are moving or have moving parts have mechanical energy. A person running across a football field has mechanical energy. What is another example of something that demonstrates mechanical energy? _____
   _____

2. *Heat* or *thermal energy* is the energy that propels a steam engine. Thermal energy is also what pushes the piston in a car. That thermal energy comes from *chemical energy* which is defined on the next page. Thermal energy is usually the product of some other form of energy. People have thermal energy. Our bodies are warm and that warmth can be used to warm other things. When we exercise, we produce more thermal energy.

   To see thermal energy work, you will need scissors, 18" of thread, a smooth piece of aluminum foil, and a lamp. Trace the pattern at the right to make a spiral shape out of the aluminum foil. (Place the foil under the pattern and draw over the dark lines. The pattern will appear on the foil.) Cut on the dark lines and make a small hole at the dot. Tie one end of the thread through this hole. Hold the spiral over the hot bulb of the lamp. What happens? _____

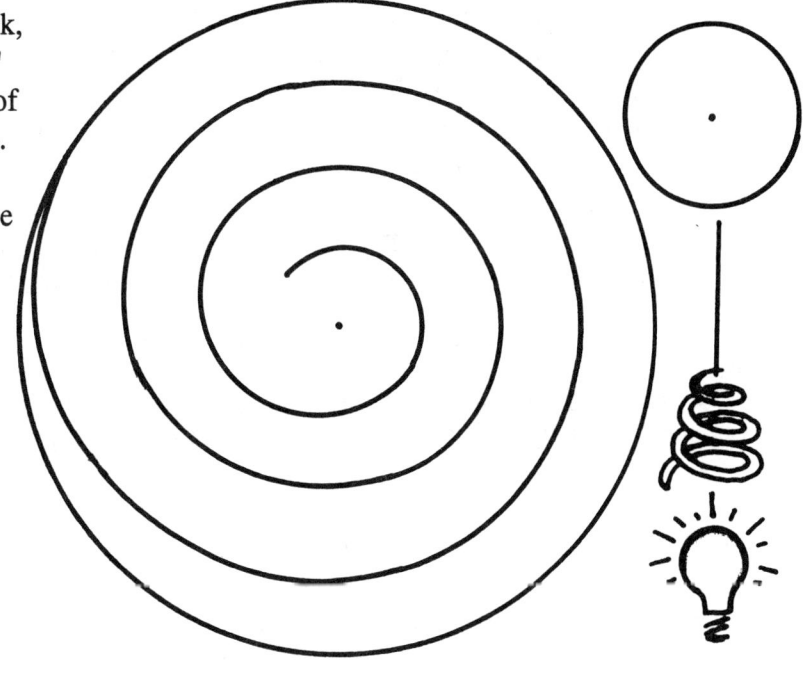

3. *Electric energy* comes from electricity. We harness electricity to run many kinds of compound machines. What are some machines that are run by electricity? _____
   _____

4. *Radiant energy* is energy which travels in rays. *Solar energy,* or energy from the sun, is one form of radiant energy. We are trying to develop ways to use more solar energy instead of using chemical energy, nuclear energy, and electrical energy. What are some ways we can already use solar energy? _____

5. *Chemical energy* is the energy from chemical reactions. Any fire is an example of chemical energy. Anything that is burning is releasing chemical energy. Any time compounds are broken down into their individual atoms or a different combination of atoms, chemical energy is released. The food you eat is broken down by the digestive process in your body. This is an example of chemical energy. Changing your food into other chemicals needed for your body results in chemical energy, which is converted by your body into heat energy or mechanical energy. The stored chemical energy in food is measured in *calories*. Your body needs a certain number of calories per day to keep you alive. If you take in too many calories, your body stores them as fat. How can you use up the extra calories if you are overweight? _____

6. What form of energy are you demonstrating when you exercise? _____

7. *Nuclear energy* comes from the splitting of atoms in a process called *fission*. This is a very powerful form of energy. It has become very controversial because the waste products of nuclear reactions are difficult to dispose of, and nuclear energy can be very dangerous when it is out of control. Another form of nuclear energy comes from the combining of atoms. This form of nuclear energy is always combined with intense heat and is called *thermonuclear*. Scientists believe the sun is an ongoing thermonuclear reaction. The atom bomb is another example of this form of energy. What forms of energy are the byproducts of thermonuclear energy? _____

8. *Elastic potential energy* is the energy in a stretched rubber band. This is also the energy in a tightly coiled spring. What can this energy be used for? _____

9. *The law of the conservation of energy* states that energy cannot be created or destroyed. If energy is lost in one form, it is increased in another form. For instance, when a car runs, it is using chemical energy and producing mechanical and heat energy. If the car is parked so it cannot produce mechanical energy, the heat energy builds up. On a hot summer day, cars stopped in a traffic jam often overheat because the heat energy builds up. Why don't the cars overheat when they are moving? _____

Electric Charge

All atoms contain protons, electrons, and neutrons. The neutrons are heavy and large, but electrically neutral. They do not have a *charge*. Protons have a positive charge but they do not leave the atom. They are in the nucleus and stay with the neutrons. The electrons orbiting the nucleus are the mobile particles.

Originally, each atom is electrically *neutral*. The number of protons is the same as the number of electrons, so the *net charge* is zero. If atoms rub against one another, some of these electrons rub off and become attached to other atoms. The atoms with extra electrons have a *negative* charge. The atoms which lose electrons have a *positive* charge.

1. Does an atom with a positive charge have more protons or more electrons? (Hint: Remember that atoms which are neutral and have not lost any electrons have an equal number of protons and electrons.)

   _____

   _____

2. Does an atom with a negative charge have more protons or more electrons? _____

   _____

Rub an inflated latex balloon with a piece of plastic wrap. Electrons will rub off the plastic wrap and onto the balloon.

3. What kind of charge does the balloon have? _____

4. What kind of charge does the plastic wrap have? _____

5. When an object becomes charged, it holds the charge until the charge can be moved to another object. The charge will move when it is transferred through **static discharge.** Can you think of a very large and powerful example of static discharge? _____

Static Electricity

Objects with an electric charge can exert a force on other charged objects. Objects with an electric charge can either *repel* or *attract* each other. If they repel each other, they push apart. Objects that attract each other pull closer together.

Materials: Two inflated latex balloons, two foot-long pieces of string, and plastic wrap

Procedure:
1. Tie one piece of string to each balloon. Rub each balloon with plastic wrap. Hold the ends of the strings so the two balloons swing free with their sides just touching. What happens? _____

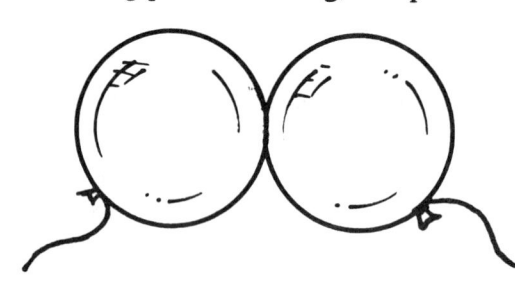

2. Rub one balloon again with the same piece of plastic wrap. Hold the balloon by the string and hold the plastic wrap two inches from the balloon. What happens? _____
_____

3. The balloons have the same charge (negative). What happens when objects with the same charge are brought close together? _____

4. The balloon and the plastic wrap have opposite charges. The balloon is negative and the plastic wrap is positive. What happens when unlike or opposite charged objects are brought close together? _____

5. In other words, you can say that like charges _____ and unlike charges _____.

This experiment has also demonstrated *electric fields*. All electrically charged objects have an electric field, which is the area around the object that contains the electrical forces that you observe. If you hold the balloons too far apart or hold the balloon too far from the plastic wrap, you will not observe any reaction because the objects are out of each others' electric fields.

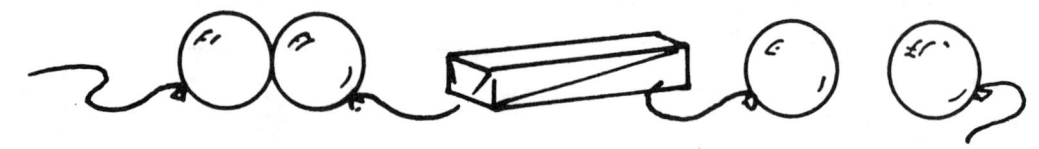

© Instructional Fair • TS Denison   IF2716 Physical Science

Conductors

Electrons can move more easily through some materials than others. Materials which allow the electrons to move easily are called *conductors*. Materials which block the flow of electrons or do not allow the electrons to move easily through them are called *insulators*.

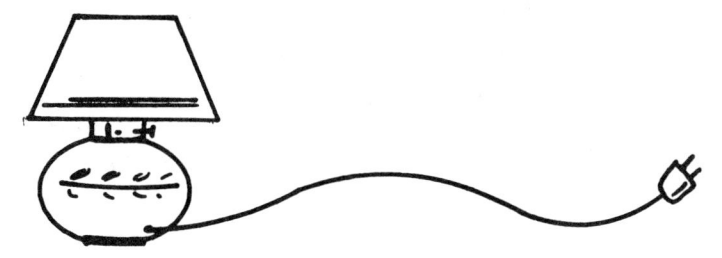

1. Look at the cord to a lamp. Can you think of one material that is a good insulator?
   _____
   _____

2. Look at the material inside a lamp cord. What kinds of material might be good conductors? _____
   _____

3. Why is the outside of the lamp cord covered with an insulating material? _____
   _____

4. Lightning is one type of very large and dangerous static discharge. Lightning bolts contain huge quantities of electrical energy. When this energy is transferred to an object on the ground, it can be very damaging. To counter this, tall buildings and buildings on high, open hills often have lightning rods. Lightning rods are made of metal and are connected to thick metal cables which run all the way to the ground. The rods conduct the electricity from the lightning to the ground. When electricity is conducted to the earth through a pathway like this, it is called *grounding*. What kinds of materials make good grounds?_____
   _____

5. Is a material that is a good ground a conductor or an insulator? _____
   _____

Electric Current

Televisions, radios, toasters, lights, and many other household items run on *electric current*. Electric current is the continuous flow of electrons from a source. Static electricity is also the movement of electrons from a source, but this transfer is done very quickly and all the electrons move at one time, so little work can be done. To have a current, electrons must flow through the conductor continuously. This happens because of a *potential difference* which is also called *voltage* (V). This can happen when there are many extra electrons at one point and a great shortage at the other point. The potential difference is measured in *volts*. Electric current can be measured in *amperes* (A). This is the rate of flow of electrons from a source.

Batteries and generators are the two main sources of electric current. A battery has two terminals, one negative and one positive. The electrons freed by a chemical reaction flow out of the negative terminal and through a conductor to the appliance. They power the appliance and then flow out through a second conductor and back to the positive terminal of the battery, which is lacking electrons. This is called *direct current* because the electric current flows only one way. Look at the battery diagram below. The battery is connected to a light bulb. Draw arrows on the diagram to show the direction of the current.

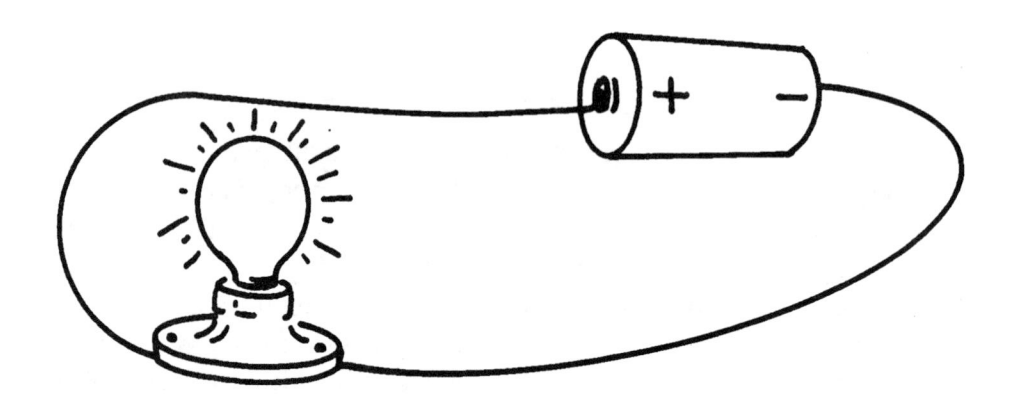

1. If you have an appliance that says to use DC, what kind of current does it use? ____

_____

2. If the chemical reaction in the battery slows down and the electrons do not flow out of the positive terminal, what happens to the electric current? _____

_____

Circuits

Any time a current flows from a source through a conductor and back to the source, you have a *closed circuit*. Look at the pictures below. Which one shows a closed circuit, A or B?

A.

B.

If the closed circuit flows from the source on a single path with no branches, that is a *series circuit*. If the conductors are running parallel to each other so the current can flow through two or more separate paths at the same time, we call it a *parallel circuit*. Label the series circuit and the parallel circuit below.

C.

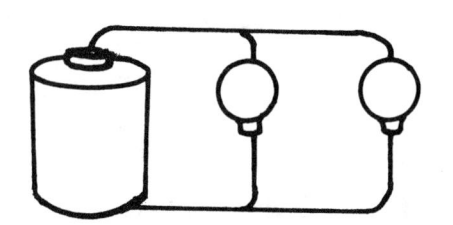

D.

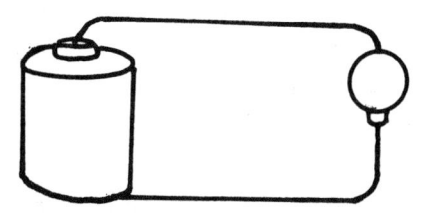

1. If lights are strung in series in a circuit as shown above, what happens if a light bulb burns out? _____

_____

A *switch* is a device that controls the flow of electrons through a circuit. When the switch is "on," the circuit is closed and the electrons can flow through the complete circuit. When the switch is "off," the circuit is not closed, and the electrons are blocked because they have no conductor to flow through. Look at the pictures below.

2. Which picture shows the switch in the "on" position? _____

E.

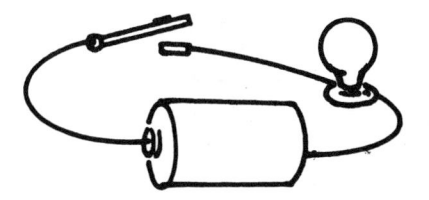

F.

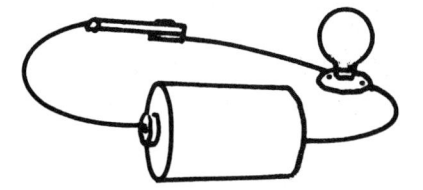

Measuring Electricity

Electrical appliances such as toasters convert electric energy into other usable forms of energy. For example, the toaster converts electricity to heat energy to cook your toast. The rate at which the toaster converts electric power to heat energy is called the *electric power* of the toaster. The *watt* is the unit used to measure electric power. Look at a light bulb. Do you see a number followed by a "W" at the end of the light bulb? That is how many watts of electric power that light bulb needs to keep it lighted.

1. Some bulbs are labeled 25W or 60W or 150W. Which one uses the most electric power? _____

2. What could you do to make a lamp containing a 150W bulb use less electric power? _____

If you know how many amperes or amps of current an appliance uses and the voltage of the current, you can calculate the power used by the appliance using this formula:

I = current
V = voltage   P = V x I
P = power

3. If a computer uses 25.5 amps of current and it is plugged into 120 volts of current (the normal household outlet), what is the power the computer uses? The computer uses _____ watts.

4. The electric company charges you for electricity based on the number of watts of electricity you use in an hour. The standard of measurement they use is kilowatt hours. One kilowatt hour (kWh) is 1,000 watts of power used in one hour. An electric company might charge you nine cents per kilowatt hour. A little meter on your house records how much electricity you use in a month. The meter reader records the number on this meter each month. The company subtracts last month's reading from this month's reading and then multiplies the answer by nine cents to figure out how much to charge you. If last month's reading is 103487 and this month's reading is 106238, how many kilowatt hours of electricity have you used this month? _____

5. At nine cents per kilowatt hour, how much will you have to pay the electric company this month? _____

Waves

1. Water, light, and sound all move in waves. Water waves are easiest to observe, but all three kinds of waves have similar properties. A wave is caused by *vibrations*. A vibration is the back-and-forth movement of particles of matter. *Mechanical waves* are waves that can travel only through matter. Sound waves are this kind of wave. You cannot have a sound wave if you do not have air or water or some other substance to carry the sound. What is another example of a mechanical wave? _____

   Electromagnetic waves do not need to travel through matter. Light, microwaves, radio waves, x-rays, and gamma rays are examples of electromagnetic waves.

2. Waves can move in one of two ways. *Transverse waves* move at right angles to the source of the wave. Fill a sink half full of water. Push the surface of the water gently with your hand. Do the bumpy little waves go up and down as in diagram A or sideways as in diagram B? _____

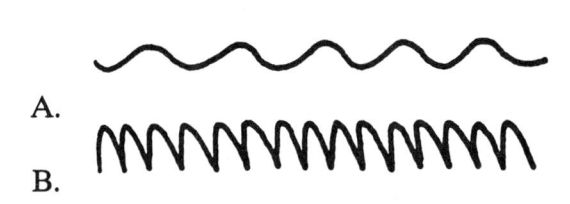

3. Matter in *compressional* or *longitudinal waves* moves in the same direction as the source. Line up five marbles in a row so they are touching one another. Push the first marble. What happens to the other four marbles? Do they bounce up and down like water waves, or do they roll out in a straight line? _____
   This is an example of a compressional wave. This is the sort of wave you find in a spring or a slinky toy. A sound wave is a compressional wave. The air molecules are pushed close together or compressed, and they in turn compress the molecules next to them.

4. To measure a wave, you must first find the *wavelength*. This is the distance from one *wave crest* (or very highest wave point) to the next wave crest or from one *wave trough* (or the very lowest point) to the next wave trough. The *amplitude* is half the height of the wave from crest to trough. Label the parts of a wave in the diagram below.

Waves

5. The amplitude of a wave is directly related to the energy of the wave. Push gently on the surface of the water in the sink. Is the wave small or large? _____

6. Push harder on the surface of the water in the sink. Is the wave small or large?
_____

7. If you increase the energy of the wave, what happens to the amplitude of the wave?
_____

8. The *frequency* is the number of waves that pass by a given point in one second. A Hertz (Hz) is the unit of measurement for frequency. One Hertz equals one wave passing by the point in one second. Would you have a higher frequency (more waves passing by point A) when the wave has a shorter wavelength (distance from crest to crest or trough to trough) or a longer wavelength? _____

9. Sound waves are caused by the vibrations of the source. When you speak, your vocal chords vibrate. Place your fingers on the front of your neck and then hum or speak. What do you feel? _____

10. The *pitch,* or how high or low the sound appears, is due to the frequency and wavelength of the sound wave. Lower frequencies and longer wavelengths produce lower sounds. People hear sounds in the 20 to 20,000 Hz frequency range. Some animals, such as bats, can hear frequencies up to the 100,000 Hz range. Can bats hear sounds with a longer or shorter wavelength than we can hear? _____
_____

11. Radio waves are measured in kiloHertz (AM radio) and megaHertz (FM radio). A kiloHertz is 1,000 wavelengths per second. A megaHertz is 1,000,000 wavelengths per second. How many wavelengths per second is a radio frequency on the FM band of 99.5 megaHertz? _____

12. How many wavelengths per second is a radio frequency on the AM band of 101.2 kiloHertz? _____

Sound levels are measured in *decibels* (dB). Waves with a higher energy level and a higher amplitude are louder. Sounds measuring higher than 120 dB can be painful to hear. Sounds measuring 95 dB or higher can damage your ears if you listen to the sounds for extended periods of time. For instance, you should not listen to sounds of 110 decibels for more than one half hour a day.

Light

Radio waves, television waves, radar waves, microwaves, infrared heat rays, visible light, ultraviolet rays, x-rays, gamma rays, and cosmic rays are all part of the wide range of electromagnetic waves known as the *electromagnetic spectrum*. Radio waves travel the most slowly and have the longest wavelength. Cosmic rays have the highest frequency and the shortest wavelength. Visible light falls in the middle of the spectrum.

Visible light is made up of bands of light of different frequencies. You can see the separate bands of light for yourself.

Materials: A clear drinking glass full of water, a ruler, a pencil, one sheet of construction paper, one sheet of white paper, tape, and scissors

Procedure:

1. Cut the sheet of construction paper so it is the same height and four inches wider than the glass. Cut a slit one-half inch wide down the center of the construction paper, leaving at least one-half inch of paper at the top and the bottom of the slit. Tape the paper to the side of the glass.

2. Place the glass in the sun so the sunlight shines through the slit in the paper. Place the white paper in front of the glass so the light coming through the slit shines directly on the white paper. What do you see? _____

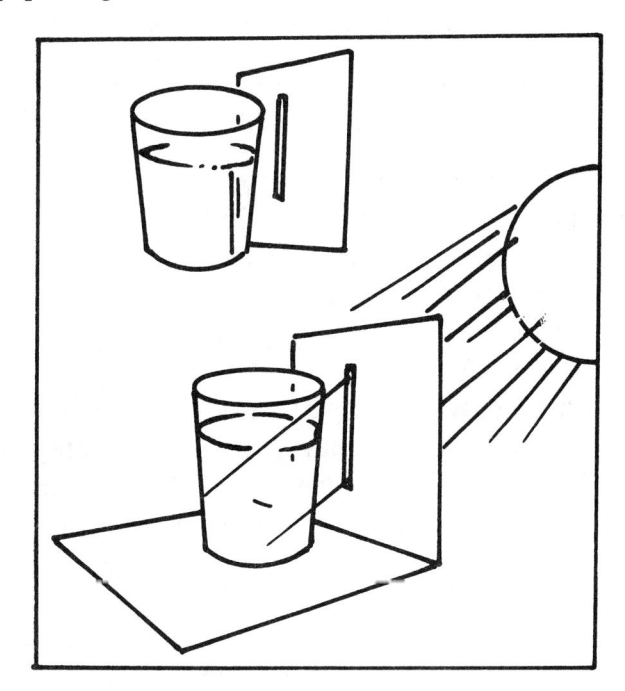

3. Color the bands of the spectrum you see in the space below. Red light has the lowest frequency and the longest wavelength. What color has the highest frequency and the shortest wavelength? _____

Lenses

1. Fill a clean, clear glass half full of water. Insert a pencil into the water. Look through the side of the glass. What seems to happen to the pencil when it enters the water?

   _____
   _____

2. This bending of light is called *refraction*. It is caused by the difference in density between the air and the water. The light travels at a different speed through the water than through the air. Light also travels at a different speed when it goes through glass. Look through a magnifying glass. What happens? _____
   _____

3. Look at the surface of the magnifying glass. Is it thicker in the center or at the edges?
   _____
   _____

4. If you cut through the center of the magnifying glass, which of the shapes at the right would represent a cross-section of the magnifying glass? _____

   A.   B.

5. A magnifying or *convex* lens bends the light as it comes through the lens. Fill a clean, clear glass with water. Cut three one-fourth-inch wide slits in the center of an index card. Darken the room. Hold the index card up to the glass and shine a flashlight through the slits in the card. What happens to the light? _____
   _____

6. A *concave* lens is the opposite of a magnifying glass. It is thin in the middle and thick on the sides. What do you think this might do to the light? Test your hypothesis if you have a concave lens to use. _____
   _____

7. A convex lens is used in the eyeglasses of farsighted people. Farsighted people need help seeing things that are close to them. What are concave lenses used for? _____

Reflections

1. Look in a mirror. What do you see? _____
   _____

Your image, called a *reflection*, occurs because the light rays that strike the mirror are being bounced back or *reflected* to your eyes.

Materials: Two or more mirrors, a sheet of construction paper, an index card, scissors, tape, and a flashlight

Procedure:
1. Cut a small hole in the center of the index card. Tape the card to the front of the flashlight so only a small beam of light shines through the hole.

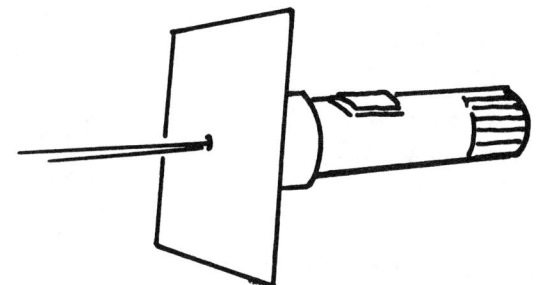

2. Prop up the mirrors and place the flashlight so the light shines onto one mirror and then is bounced onto the other mirror and then bounces onto the sheet of construction paper. Darken the room to help you see the light beams more clearly. Draw the positions of the mirrors, the flashlight, and the paper in the space below when you get the setup to work.

3. Sound and other waves can be reflected. Auditoriums and sound stages are built in special shapes to reflect the sound waves. Satellite dishes and radar receivers are dish-shaped to condense the waves that hit the surface of the dish instead of reflecting them. Look at the diagram below. Where do the waves go? _____

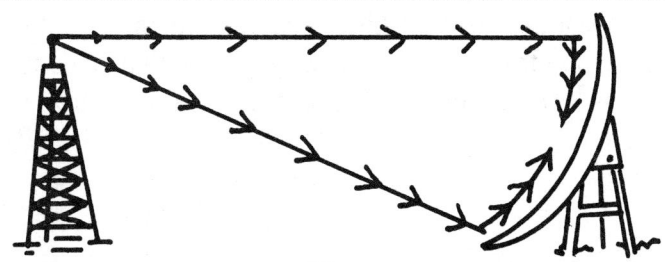

Interference

When waves cross each other, they combine in some places and cancel each other out in others. This is called *interference*.

Materials: Two index cards, scissors, tape, two flashlights, and a large sheet of white posterboard

Procedure:
1. Cut five one-eighth inch wide parallel slits in each index card. Make the slits close enough and short enough to cover the inside of the flashlight lenses as in the diagram to the right.

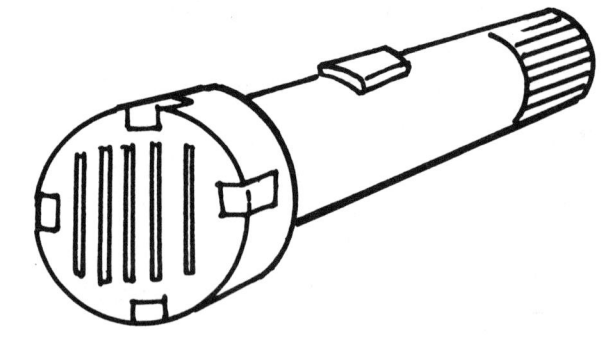

2. Tape the index cards to the front of the flashlights. Place the two flashlights side by side at the edge of the posterboard. Turn the flashlights on and darken the room. Draw the pattern that you see in the space below.

Another interesting effect is the *Doppler effect*. This occurs when a sound is moving toward or away from an observer. If you listen closely to a train or an ambulance as it comes toward you, the sound of the whistle or siren seems to get higher in pitch. The sound lowers again as the train or ambulance passes by you. This is because the waves compress as the sound comes closer and spread out as they go away from you.

Answer Key

Measuring — Page 1
The meter, the liter, and the ounce are larger.
1. 52 feet
2. three times
3. 24 cups
4. one liter
The metric problems are easier to solve because they are in units of ten and require less multiplication and division.

Measurement Charts — Page 2
1. The prefix centi- means 1/100 of the unit.
2. The prefix milli- means 1/1000 of the unit.
3. The prefix hecto- means 100 times the unit.
4. The prefix kilo- means 1000 times the unit.

Lab Tools — Page 3
1. d
2. c
3. f
4. b
5. g
6. a
7. e

Matter — Page 4
1. M solid
2. M gas
3. M liquid
4. M liquid
5. M solid
6. M solid
7. M liquid
8. M solid
9. M solid

Substances — Page 5
Salt is a substance. Is is a crystal, large crystals are clear, small crystals appear white in color, it tastes salty... Gold is an element. It is shiny and yellow in color, malleable, it is clear when melted, it is heavy... Ice cream melted is a physical change. A log burned is a chemical change. Water evaporated is a physical change. A pancake cooked is a chemical change.

Combining Substances — Page 6
Sugar is a compound. Mercury is an element. Cinnamon and sugar are a mixture. Sugar water is a solution.

Atoms — Page 7
3a. Gold is yellow and shiny.
3b. Silver is gray and shiny.
5a. Oxygen and hydrogen combine to form water.
5b. Oxygen and hydrogen are colorless gases. Water is a clear liquid.

What Do Atoms Look Like? — Page 8
The diagram should be labeled as follows: protons, neutrons, electrons.

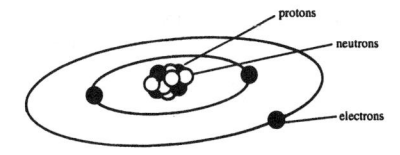

1. The atom has no net electric charge; it is zero.
2. 2,000,000 chlorine atoms would be one meter long.

What Do These Letters Mean? — Page 9
Silver Ag   Carbon C   Tin Sn
Chlorine Cl   Boron B   Arsenic As
Argon Ar   Sulfur S   Platinum Pt
Helium He   Radon Rn   Neon Ne

Ammonium nitrate: two nitrogen, two hydrogen, two oxygen
Potassium chlorate: one potassium, one chlorine, three oxygen
Sodium peroxide: two sodium, two oxygen
Sulfuric acid: one hydrogen, one sulfur, four oxygen
Alka-Seltzer: one sodium, one hydrogen, one carbon, three oxygen
Tums: one calcium, one carbon, three oxygen

Atomic Numbers — Page 11
carbon 6, calcium 20, oxygen 8
1. Au is gold. It has 79 protons and 79 electrons.
2. C is carbon. It has 6 protons and 6 electrons.

The Periodic Table — Page 12
1. Copper (Cu) is used to make pennies.
2. Arsenic (As) is often used in pesticides.
3. Sodium (Na) and chlorine (Cl) are the halogens in salt.
4. Helium (He) is often used to inflate balloons.
5. Neon (Ne) is often used in lights.

Molecules — Page 14
Ethylene (C_2H_4) is a compound. Carbon monoxide (CO) is a compound. Carbon dioxide (CO_2) is a compound. Oxygen (O) is an element.

Ions — Page 15
1. Al, Aluminum
2. 23 electrons, 26 protons, iron
3. 36 electrons, 34 protons, selenium

What Is Special About Ions — Page 16
1. Na^{+1}
2. Cl^{-1}
3. NaCl
4. $AlCl_3$
It contains aluminum and chlorine.
5. Al_2O_3

Organic Compounds — Page 17
1. Organic
2. Inorganic
3. Inorganic
4. Organic
5. Organic
6. Water is commonly found in living organisms.
7. All three are flammable gases used for heating, cooking, and fuel.

Chemical Equations — Page 18
1. $2Al + 6HCl \longrightarrow 2AlCl_3 + 3H_2$
2. $CH_4 + 2O_2 \longrightarrow CO_2 + 2H_2O$
3. $2K + 2H_2O \longrightarrow 2NaOH + H$

© Instructional Fair • TS Denison   IF2716 Physical Science

4. Potassium (K) is a solid, water (H$_2$O) is a liquid, KOH is a liquid, and H is a gas.
5. 1 Na + 2H$_2$O $\longrightarrow$ 2NaOH + H$_2$

Solutions Page 19
There is no difference in the taste.
1. Pepsi is a solution.
2. Seawater is a solution.
3. An oil slick is not a solution.
4. A chocolate chip cookie is not a solution.
5. A glass of Kool-aid is a solution.
6. Water is the solvent.
7. Sugar is the solute.
8. Seawater is an aqueous solution.

Electrolytess Page 20
1. Ammonium chloride and manganese dioxide are electrolytes.
2. Teapots, jewelry, silverware, picture frames, belt buckles, and coins are eleroplated. Silver, copper, and gold are often used to plate these items.
3. Hard water would be a better conductor of electricity.

Concentrations Page 21
1. This is a weak concentration. It is not sweet.
2. This is a strong concentration. It is very sweet.
3. The hot water will hold more sugar.
4. You could heat the water to make it dissolve the solute more quickly and to hold more solute.

Making Crystals Page 22
2. Crystals form in the dishes as the water absorbs.
3. All of the crystals have different shapes.

Chemical Reactions Page 23
1. It would feel cold.
2. The plaster of Paris can feels warm. It is an ectothermic reaction.
3. C$_3$H$_{8(g)}$ + 5O$_{2(g)}$ $\longrightarrow$ CO$_{2(g)}$ + 4H$_2$O$_{(l)}$
4. The oxygen and the propane are gases.
5. The carbon dioxide is a gas; the water is a liquid.
A. Ectothermic   B. Endothermic

Catalysts Page 24
1. The hydrogen peroxide bubbles and the liver changes color.
2. The match relights
3. The bubbles from the hydrogen peroxide are oxygen gas.

Qualitative Analysis Page 25
1. Potato and bread are starches.
2. The spoon turns black where the rubber band touched it.
3. The teaspoon turns black where the egg touched it. The egg contains sulfur.
4. You could place it in direct contact with an item that contains sulfur.

Acids Page 26
Turmeric indicator: clear
Red cabbage indicator: pink
Phenolphthalein indicator: tan

Bases Page 27
1. Litmus paper: blue
   Turmeric indicator: bright yellow
   Red cabbage indicator: blue, blue-green
   Phenolphthalein indicator: pink
2. Your results indicate whether the substance is acid or base.
3. The indicator changes back to the color for a base.
4. Dip them in the opposite substance.
5. Water does not change the color of the indicator.

Precipitates Page 28
1. Small flakes form and drift to the bottom of the glass.
2. The glass bubbles; then the mixture gets cloudy.
3. A precipitate has formed at the bottom of the glass.
4. Antacids all do basically the same. They all form precipitates.

Isotopes Page 29
1. 17 protons and 20 neutrons
2. 79 protons and 118 neutrons
3. 19 protons and 18 neutrons
4. 18 protons and 22 neutrons

Force Page 30
1. Force is changing the direction of the soccer ball.
2. Force is pushing the ball upward.
3. Force is stopping the ball.
4. Force is increasing the speed of the bike.
5. Gravitation

Magnetism Page 31
1. The hanging magnet changes direction.
2. The needle of the compass lines up in the opposite direction of the magnet.
3. The compass needle turns the other way.
4. The pole labeled north but with the opposite electrical charge of the earth's north pole.
5. The lines of magnetic force should make the filings form this pattern:

6. Yes, it has a different pattern.
7. Iron is the metal attracted to magnets. No other metals are attracted to magnets.

Electromagnets Page 32
Electromagnets are used in industry to lift very heavy steel and iron objects such as old car bodies.
4. When the compass comes near the nail, the needle moves.
5. The compass needle turns the other way.
6. The nail has become a magnet (an electromagnet).
7. The magnetism disappears when the battery is disconnected.

Other Kinds of Force   Page 33
1. Friction allows us to control the speed and direction of ourselves and other objects.
2. Friction makes it harder to move things; it opposes motion.
3. The Styrofoam pieces fly away.
4. Your hair moves toward the balloon.
5. The balloon has a negative charge.

Are Forces Always Balanced?   Page 34
1. In outer space things keep moving until they hit something.
2. 1 foot
3. The moon's gravitational force is ⅙ that of earth's.
4. It would take more force to launch a rocket on Jupiter because the gravitational force is greater.

The Laws of Motion   Page 35
1. The wind could blow it, a person or animal could push it, an earthquake could shake it.
2. The car moves forward; it accelerates.
3. If you push hard forward, the swing goes a long way backward.
4. It swings forward.

Motion   Page 36
1. 8.7 km/h
2. 160 m/h
3. Wind

The Theory of Relativity   Page 37
1. Your opinion on this is as valid as anyone else's. This is theory, not fact. No one knows the answer.
2. Again, your opinion is as valid as anyone else's.

Work   Page 38
1. Placing a book on a book shelf is work. Pushing against a building is not.
2. The person lifting the weight overhead is doing more work than the person lifting the weight to his shoulders.
3. The ant moving the whole cupcake is doing more work because he is using more force to move a larger mass.

Simple Machines   Page 39
1. A teeter-totter or seesaw is a lever; a flat, manual can opener is a lever; a crowbar is a lever.
2. Stairs, ladders, ramps, and slides are all examples of inclined planes.
3. Doorknobs; steering wheels; wheels on wagons, bikes, and vehicles; and merry-go-rounds are examples of wheel and axle.
4. Pulleys can be found on clotheslines, barns, **fishing poles** and flagpoles.

Using a Simple Machine   Page 40
1. How many did you lift?
2. You should find it harder to lift the books with the long side of the ruler on the book side of the fulcrum.
3. You should be able to lift more books this way.
4. You can make the load easier to lift by changing the position of the fulcrum.

Can a Machine Be More Efficient?   Page 41
1. The oil reduces the friction between your fingers. Oil is a lubricant.
2. Smooth paper is easier to rub together.
3. The book is easier to move when it is on top of the marbles.

Energy   Page 42
1. kinetic energy
2. potential energy
3. potential energy
4. kinetic energy

Different Forms of Energy   Page 43
1. Any moving machine or appliance is an example of mechanical energy.
2. The heat energy makes the spiral spin.
3. Lights, toasters, ovens, hair dryers, and many other appliances are run by electricity.
4. Radiant energy can be used to power calculators and cars, heat houses, heat water, and power solar cells.
5. You can exercise more.
6. Exercise is mechanical energy.
7. Heat and light are byproducts of nuclear energy.
8. This can be used to pull things tight together or to propel things.
9. When cars are moving, some of the chemical energy is converted to mechanical energy.

Electric Charge   Page 45
1. An atom with a positive charge has more protons.
2. An atom with a negative charge has more electrons.
3. The balloon has a negative charge.
4. The plastic wrap has a positive charge.
5. Lightning is a very large, powerful static discharge.

Static Electricity   Page 46
1. The balloons fly apart.
2. The balloon and the plastic pull together.
3. Objects with the same charge repel each other or fly apart.
4. Objects with the opposite or unlike charges attract one another or pull together.
5. Like charges repel, unlike charges attract.

Conductors   Page 47
1. Plastic and rubber are good insulators.
2. Metals are good conductors.
3. The insulation keeps the charge from flowing through you or other objects the wire touches.
4. Good conductors (metals) make good grounds.
5. A good ground is a conductor.

Electric Current   Page 48
The diagram should look like this:

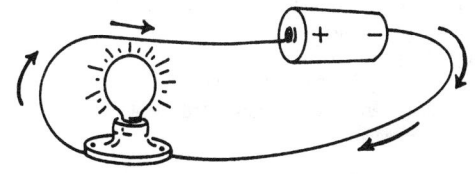

1. DC is direct current.
2. The electric current stops flowing.

Circuits   **Page 49**
A is a closed circuit. C is a parallel circuit. D is a series circuit.
1. If one bulb in a series burns out, the whole string of lights goes out.
2. E is off. F is on.

Measuring Electricity   **Page 50**
1. The 150W bulb uses the most power.
2. You could use a lower-watt bulb.
3. 3060 watts
4. 2751 kilowatt hours
5. $247.59

Waves   **Page 51**
1. Water is another mechanical wave.
2. The waves go up and down as in diagram A.
3. Marbles roll out in a straight line.
4. The diagram should be labeled as follows:

                                          Page 52
5. The wave is small.
6. The wave is large.
7. The amplitude increases.
8. When the wave has a shorter wavelength, it has a higher frequency.
9. You feel the vibrations of your vocal chords.
10. Bats can hear sounds with a shorter wavelength.
11. 99,500,00 wavelengths per second
12. 101,200 wavelengths per second

Light   **Page 53**
2. You see a rainbow or a spectrum of the colors of light.
3. The band should be colored in the following order:

        red orange yellow green blue violet

(You may include the color indigo between blue and violet.)

Lenses   **Page 54**
1. The pencil appears to be bent.
2. The object appears larger.
3. A magnifying glass is thicker in the middle.
4. It would be shaped like A.
5. The light converges or comes together.
6. A concave lens spreads the light out.
7. Concave lenses are used for nearsighted people to help them see distant objects.

Reflections   **Page 55**
1. You see your image or reflection.
2. The diagram might look like this:
3. The waves in a satellite dish bounce off the edges and are reflected to the center of the dish.

Interference   **Page 56**
The pattern should look like this: